TO JEFF CARRETIE

IN MEMORY OF YOUR FATHER, ONE
OF THE FINEST GENTLEMAN I HAVE
EVER KNOWN

Larry Tracy
Col. USA (Ret)
MAY 9, 2013

To my wife Fely

Knowing I am happier in front of an audience than behind a keyboard, she encouraged and cajoled me to write this book. Without her, it would not have been written. For that I am so very grateful, as I hope will be all readers.

Table of Contents

Part I
The Art of the Persuasive Presentation

Part II
Planning

Part III
Practicing

Part IV
Presenting

Part V
Applying the *S3P3 System* to Special Situations

About the Author

Larry Tracy conducts presentation skills workshops for corporate executives and government officials. He is a retired U.S. Army colonel with extensive speaking experience under difficult conditions. He formerly headed the Pentagon's top briefing team, responsible for daily intelligence presentations to the Chairman of the Joint Chiefs of Staff, the Secretary of Defense and other Defense Department officials.

Because of his reputation for exceptional speaking ability, the State Department requested the Army to assign him to State for the specific purpose of explaining and debating controversial foreign policy issues. He proceeded to speak and debate almost 400 times before some of the most demanding, even hostile, audiences in the country. His executive workshops, and this book, flow from this real–world experience.

He is a graduate of St. Joseph's University in Philadelphia, holds an MA from Georgetown University and is a graduate of the U.S. Army Command & Staff College and the Inter–American Defense College.

Testimonials

"You have been a splendid spokesman for America... an extraordinarily effective speaker... meeting with hundreds of audiences at the White House and in communities across the country, as well as abroad."

President Ronald Reagan

"In a Department that prides itself on its communication skills, you became the standard to match in public oratory."

Ambassador Otto Reich,
U.S. Department of State

"Larry Tracy is one of the most articulate advocates I've ever seen operate on the platform. He's crisp and clear, his logic and thinking first–rate. As a speech coach myself, I continue to learn from him."

John Jay Daly,
Founder,
National Capital Speakers Association

"You not only trained twenty–two people how to speak convincingly in some fairly hostile situations, but in two cases your training actually changed personalities."

Steven Cox,
Director, Office of Intelligence and Threat Analysis.
U.S. Department of State

"I have been trying cases for over thirty years, and have given a number of legal papers. It was surprising to me how much your training contributed to my presentation ability."

Carl G. Love,
Partner, Cushman, Darby and Cushman,
Attorneys at Law, Washington D.C.

"You provided an excellent learning experience to the Department of Defense Executive Leadership Development Program. The advice on dealing with difficult groups, and the delivery techniques demonstrated, prepared participants for future briefings they will be required to present."

Warren L. Banes, Jr.,
Acting Director, Executive Leadership Development Program,
Office of the Secretary of Defense

ix

"In my years of experience in training and development, I have never read more enthusiastic seminar evaluations. You showed our people how to convert arcane and complex technical information into a clear and persuasive presentation."

Bill Fender,
Manager, Human Resources,
LOGICON Operating Systems, Arlington, VA

"Your seminar on "Advocacy" for NASA Program and Project Managers was one of the best I have seen in my professional experience."

Francis Hoban*,*
Manager,
NASA Program and Project Manager Training Initiative

"Thanks again for the first−rate training seminar you provided our economists... the clarity of our message and the professional image of WEFA as the premier economic forecasting firm in the U.S. were enhanced by your training."

Gerard Vila,
Chairman & CEO,
The WEFA Group, Philadelphia

x

Preface

"If, through some inscrutable act of providence, I were to lose all my faculties save one, I would wish to retain the gift of speech, for with it I would soon regain all the others."

Senator Daniel Webster

What Senator Webster said in the 19th Century is just as valid today: Strong presentation skills are the key to achievement and success. The ability to express oneself is among the most important skills for those in business or government aspiring to senior positions, while the inability to communicate is often a career–stopper.

An audience, whether it is one person or many, wants speakers to provide *maximum* relevant information, delivered in *minimum* time and in the *clearest* possible terms, centered on the needs and concerns of the audience.

If you want to deliver this kind of presentation, but are constantly pressed for time, you need an easy–to–learn–and–implement method to create and deliver presentations that are memorable and persuasive.

That is precisely what you will gain from this book. It is based on the assumption that people who must develop strong presentation skills, but lack the time to learn all the "glitz" of the professional speaker, require a *shortcut* system.

In the business world, millions of dollars in contracts often turn on the effectiveness of the sales presentation, not the merits of the product or service. Consequently, those who can distill and explain complex data in "pressure–cooker" situations (such as boardroom presentations for project funding or competitive presentations for lucrative contracts) are highly valued. Moreover, when called on to speak extemporaneously at meetings, you have a wonderful opportunity to shine and to impress. You also have a wonderful opportunity to fall on your face if you cannot deliver a hard–hitting, succinct message.

By following the system developed in this book, you will indeed learn to organize and deliver your expertise, focused on meeting the needs and solving the problems of various "audiences." Clients, customers, Boards of Directors, shareholders, etc. will conclude that what you are proposing is in their best interests, and that you are an outstanding speaker.

Keep in mind that every presentation is actually four presentations: (1) the one you plan to deliver, (2) the one you actually deliver, (3) the one your audience hears you deliver, and (4) the one you wish you had delivered. After internalizing the systematic, proven approach in this book, you will be able to deliver as you have planned and practiced, be on the same page as the audience, and have fewer of those *"I wish I had said it this way"* moments.

What about the well–known fear of public speaking? Survey after survey ranks "speaking in front of a group" at or near the top in lists of phobias. Even as this book was going to press, the July 7, 2003 issue of *Business Week* published the results of a recent survey of managers which asked what work–related activities made them most uncomfortable. *"Speaking to large audiences"* ranked behind only *"building relationships with people I dislike"* and *"asking for a raise."*

Unlike many speech coaches, I make no promises that merely reading my book will vanquish your apprehension about speaking to groups. Nor do I believe you should seek to eliminate this fear, which can be used to develop energy and enthusiasm. What I do promise is a system which will reduce the fear of the unknown, the underlying cause of the fear of public speaking.

Let's start this *shortcut* to becoming a persuasive and eloquent presenter at an unlikely place – a comic strip. In March 2002, the strip *Beetle Bailey* contained a valuable insight for presenters. As General Halftrack walked into his office, his secretary asked: *"How was Lt. Fuzz's presentation?"*

The General replied: *"Like the Washington Monument."* Puzzled, the secretary asked *"The Washington Monument?"* The General responded, *"Yeah, it took a long time to get to the point."*

How often have you felt the same frustration of General Halftrack because the speaker didn't "get to the point?" Worse, have people listening to your presentations been exasperated because they didn't know where you were taking them, didn't know what was your point?

What about all those books promising to impart the secrets of public speaking? The advice in these books is generally excellent; there is just too much of it for busy people to absorb and implement. These books are analogous to providing a thirsty person with a fire hose from which to drink.

That is why I have written the kind of book I wish I had had when I was speaking to demanding audiences throughout the country – an easy–to–learn–and–internalize system that can be adapted to a wide array of presentations. In other words, a *shortcut* system that shows how to *plan, practice* and *present* audience–centered, persuasive presentations with a minimum investment of time.

The following pages are a distillation of the lessons I learned while making hundreds of presentations on controversial issues to demanding audiences. These lessons are the bedrock of my executive training workshops, where participants learn a "real–world" and timesaving method to achieve speaking excellence and become "persuasively eloquent."

Let's look at what you will find on these pages.

In Part 1, *The Art of the Persuasive Presentation*, I explain my *S3P3* model – the pillars of Substance, Structure and Style which support the Pyramid of Planning, Practicing and Presenting.

Part II, *Planning*, shows the fundamentals of planning a presentation, especially how to organize your knowledge by structuring backwards with the 3–1–2 system. This method provides focus and thematic unity and helps you get to the point the audience is interested in hearing.

You'll learn as well techniques to gain "intelligence" on audience members so you can mesh your objective with their needs. You will also learn how to develop a *Plan B presentation* when you find you have less time to speak than you thought you had.

Part III, *Practicing*, covers the all–important process to be followed in getting ready to face your audience. The most vital element of this process is the realistic simulation called the *Murder Board*, which has its origins in the U.S. military. Don't be intimidated by the name. Such a practice session will enable you to learn from your mistakes before your actual presentation, anticipate questions, and, in general, take the fear out of speaking because you are lessening the fear of the unknown.

In Part IV, *Presenting*, the apex of the Pyramid, you will see how to convert nervousness to energy, use non–verbals to augment your oral message, and use visuals, including PowerPoint slides, so they reinforce, not distract from, your message. You'll also learn how to read a scripted presentation when you have no alternative, and how to answer questions so you drive your point home.

Part V, *Applying the S3P3 Method to Special Situations*, focuses on particularly challenging situations: Oral presentations for contracts, and the strategy and tactics of addressing audiences predisposed to disagree. Very few books on speaking provide any in–depth advice about these most daunting of speaking challenges.

If you take the *shortcut* outlined in this book, you will arrive at a level of speaking excellence where your audiences will praise your eloquence, not comment on you the way General Halftrack critiqued Lt. Fuzz.

Acknowledgments

I realize that, in a book promising to be a *"shortcut,"* this acknowledgment section is a bit lengthy. Please bear with me; not only are there many people to thank, but reading this section will give you a clearer idea about the route I will be taking you on this *"shortcut"* to speaking excellence.

Two institutions of government have had much to do with my learning the art of presenting: The U.S. Army and the Department of State. The presentations experience I gained in those two organizations provided the real world know–how contained in this book.

The Army taught me the true *shortcut* to effective speaking – the *bottom line up front* briefing. I use it in my own speaking and training, but without the starch normally found in military briefings.

Among the lessons I learned, and include in this book, was a unique practice method allowing presenters to anticipate questions and have a *Plan B* presentation always ready, indispensable skills in front of demanding audiences.

During my Army career I was fortunate to have many mentors, especially the late John Hughes, the senior civilian in the Defense Intelligence Agency (DIA), and a legend in the Intelligence Community. He knew more about briefing than any person I ever met, and kindly shared with me much of his knowledge. His advice was to always *"stay within the evidentiary base,"* which is as important for business presentations as it is for intelligence briefings.

The Army also gave me two assignments that provided intensive presentation experience by putting me on the platform daily: A three year tour as the intelligence instructor at the U.S. Army Engineer School, and a subsequent two year stint as head of the DIA Presentations Branch, where I was responsible for daily briefings to the Chairman of the Joint Chiefs of Staff and the Secretary of Defense.

During a later assignment in the Office of the Secretary of Defense, I did a great deal of speaking for the Pentagon on U.S. policy in Latin America. As a result, the State Department requested that I be detailed to the Department to speak throughout the country on controversial foreign policy issues. In the next three years, I participated in almost 400 presentations, debates and panels, many of them confrontational.

It was this experience in particular that led me to the field of speech coaching. I realized few, if any, people in this field had the first–hand experience of actually facing demanding, often hostile, audiences. I concluded the lessons I had learned the hard way could be benefit others through training workshops, and now in this book.

Moving from the institutional to the personal, I want to publicly thank my wife Fely, the linchpin of our family, for her encouragement. Without her support, I know I would never have written this book. I am grateful to her beyond words.

Our daughters, Terry, Kathleen and Margot, all excellent speakers, have been wonderfully constructive critics. They also persuaded me to change the title of the book, originally *"Presentation Skills in a Nutshell."* When it reached 180–plus pages, they protested that it had moved far beyond nutshell length, and insisted I change the title. Having learned over the years to respect their judgment, I reluctantly agreed. I'm glad I did.

My son–in–law, Dr. Patrick Baier, Terry's husband, has been pivotal in converting my abstract book concept to a concrete product. His German sense of order, Cambridge and Oxford trained mathematical precision, and in–depth computer knowledge truly enabled this book to be written. He spent almost as much time editing, proofing and formatting as I did writing. I am greatly indebted to him for his invaluable assistance.

Cathi Stevenson designed the book's eye–catching cover, which evolved over several emails. Cathi lives in Nova Scotia, Canada, and I live in Virginia. I described in general terms what I wanted, and she improved upon my ideas.

Finally, I want to thank the thousands of business executives, government officials, lawyers, engineers, military officers, diplomats, etc. who have attended my workshops. They brought to the classroom myriad challenges they had encountered in speaking to groups, many of which were new to me.

These new perspectives forced me to develop solutions I would have not have devised without such stimulation. This book is a richer source of help for all speakers because of the contributions of these people.

Part I

The Art of the
Persuasive Presentation

Chapter 1

Three Vital Questions

As social animals, we spend most of our time in oral communication with our fellow social animals. Although the written document is a more efficient means of communicating data, it is not as effective as the spoken word in writing our ideas on the brains of others.

We are accustomed to receiving information directly from human beings. That is why we watch an anchor person read the news to us from a TelePrompTer. If receiving information was our primary goal, a more efficient means of learning the data would be to have the camera directed at the TelePrompTer so we could read the text ourselves. But would we?

Because of this predisposition we have to communicate with each other face–to–face, the ability to make a coherent, convincing presentation is a vital ability for every person – in government or the private sector – who has the ambition to succeed. Let's begin by addressing three questions which are central for anyone who wishes to become a more powerful and persuasive presenter.

1.1 "Are speaking skills important?"

The very fact that you have acquired this book suggests you believe that being able to make a persuasive presentation is among the most important skills to have in business, or in life for that matter.

Many mid–level managers have seen their careers go down the tubes because of their inability to communicate in high–pressure situations. Lee Iacocca, in his years at Ford and Chrysler, was a strong advocate of intensive training in speaking skills for his engineers. Keep in mind that it was his ability to communicate, not his engineering talent, that ultimately persuaded Congress to make the loan to bail out Chrysler. Reflecting on the importance of being able to speak well, Iacocca wrote in his autobiography:

> *"I've known a lot of engineers with terrific ideas who had trouble explaining them to others. It's always a shame when a guy with great talent can't tell the board or a committee what's in his head."*

Iacocca was not the first to make this observation. He was repeating, in effect, the words of Pericles. Over 2,500 years ago, that great Greek statesman and orator said

> *"A person who can think, but cannot express what he thinks, places himself at the level of the person who cannot think."*

Don't those two statements, separated by so many centuries, just say it all about the need to develop excellent presentation skills? How many brilliant people have you seen become tongue–tied when asked to make a presentation?

How many times have you experienced the frustration of being unable to unlock the knowledge you had on a subject because you couldn't find the words, or were petrified at the prospect of speaking before a group? The result: You failed to persuade.

1.2 "Why is public speaking so feared in America?"

In October 1973, the *Sunday Times* of London asked 3,000 Americans what was their greatest fear. The results? 41% said *"speaking in front of a group,"* while 19% said *"dying."*

What is your greatest fear?

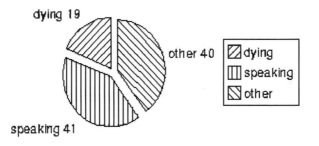

Source: *Sunday Times*, October 7, 1973.

Jerry Seinfeld used this survey in the opening of one of his programs by wondering if this meant that most people would rather be in a coffin than deliver the eulogy. Surveys in subsequent years have consistently placed *public speaking* at the top of lists of things people would rather not do.

From my experience in training business executives and government officials, I have come to the conclusion that the overarching reason many people are petrified at the prospect of speaking before a group is *fear of the unknown.* I'll address the reasons for this fear and ways to channel nervousness into positive energy in Chapter 15. You may wish to jump ahead and read that chapter before proceeding with the rest of the book.

Because of speaker anxiety, many talented and competent people avoid speaking in public and thereby choose to remain on the sidelines. Others do make presentations because they have no choice, but hide behind the fatalistic myth that speakers are born, not made. They make no effort to improve their speaking ability.

Ironically, they make the investment of time and energy to learn the complexities of computer science, engineering, the law or some other complex discipline, but remain convinced that being a good speaker is an innate talent, not one that can be acquired. How wrong they are, what a tragedy for them, what a waste of human capital for their companies!

1.3 "What is the most important characteristic for presenters to possess?"

Let me tell you first what it is not. It is not mastering *PowerPoint*, nor is it the ability to turn a clever phrase, nor a mellifluous voice and riveting eye contact.

The most important characteristic you must possess to be an effective speaker is **credibility**. The speaker who is judged credible by audience members receives the most important element in communication – trust.

Aristotle, father of public speaking training, used the Greek word *ethos* to describe this characteristic. He maintained that an audience that knows little of the subject being discussed would be inclined to accept the point being advocated if the speaker had *ethos*. In my judgment, credibility flows from the fusing of three elements:

First, the speaker's **expertise**. The audience wants to benefit by the speaker's knowledge, and therefore needs to know that the speaker has something worthwhile to say that will answer the eternal question of all audiences: *"What's in it for me?"*

Second, the speaker's **believability**. We want the speaker to give us the truth, not spin, not propaganda. If an audience perceives that the speaker is not being truthful, that speaker might just as well save his or her breath. An old saying sums up the need to be truthful: *You can't believe liars, even when they are telling the truth.*

Third, the speaker's **likeability**. Audiences – and clients – accept information from people they like, reject it from people they dislike. This is actually a fault of all of us who listen to presentations. The speaker may be an expert, may be telling the truth, but because we don't like the speaker, we tune out. In doing so, we unfortunately cut ourselves off from valuable information because of our subjective reaction.

A lesson for managers is that if you have people working for you who are experts and are truthful, but who cause the temperature to drop by ten degrees when they enter a room, make sure they work on interpersonal skills before addressing a board of directors or clients.

Let me end this chapter with what may be a surprise for many of you. No presenter can say that he or she *possesses* credibility. Credibility is *bestowed* by audience members based on how they perceive our expertise, believability, and likeability. In the next chapter, we'll set the stage for the rest of the book by outlining what I have dubbed my *S3P3 System.*

Chapter 2

The *S3P3 System*

Being able to express yourself is the best way to stand out from the crowd. The famed management expert Peter Drucker has written that

> *"the ability to express oneself is perhaps the most important of all the skills a person can possess."*

While the thrust of this book is communicating effectively and efficiently to groups, the advice in these pages has equal applicability to one–on–one communications. The principles remain the same, whether one is speaking to one person or a thousand people.

Effective, persuasive communication is transferring information from your brain to the brains(s) of your audience in such a manner that this audience – one or many – accepts your information as its own.

This requires focus, thematic unity, and an in–depth knowledge of what motivates your audience so you can direct your message to hit these *hot buttons*. It also requires the ability to anticipate objections and questions the audience may have, and the discipline to practice realistically.

To be an effective speaker, one must certainly know his/her stuff. That is almost a truism, although there are many people with more audacity than judgment who stand before a group with far less knowledge than prudence would dictate.

The majority of people who are called on to present, however, are substantive experts, and therein lies an essential problem. They believe that technical knowledge is sufficient, and they need not devote any attention to delivery skills, for they consider themselves neither actors nor *talking dogs*.

The intellectual underpinning of this book is that there are three essential pillars of any presentation:

- *Substance,* the knowledge of the subject being presented;
- *Structure,* the arrangement of ideas and words which makes the message understandable to the audience because it is delivered in the manner that the human mind processes data;
- *Style,* the passion and verve of the speaker – the use of rhetorical devices, the effective use of non–verbals such as voice inflection, eye contact, and the use of positive (and the avoidance of negative) body language.

The three–stage Pyramid – *Planning, Practicing* and *Presenting* – is the model this book will outline, and it may be helpful to view this Pyramid as supported by these three pillars. If one of the pillars collapses, the Pyramid falls.

2.1 Substance

Mastery of the subject is an absolute necessity for any speaker. You must have a clearly defined *objective* and focused *research*. This does not mean only compilation of factual data. You need an *active* and comprehensive knowledge of the subject at issue in order to respond to challenges from the audience, especially if the audience may be predisposed to disagree.

Only a solid grasp of the subject matter can save a presenter when confronted with an unexpected question or objection from the audience. However, *Substance* without *Structure* or *Style* can make the presentation an incoherent, boring recitation of data.

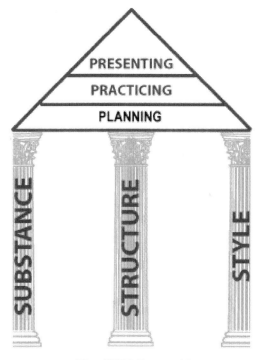

The S3P3 Pyramid

2.2   Structure

The human mind possesses a certain data–processing logic. The speaker who is aware of how people process information, and how new data is either accepted or rejected, can learn to structure a presentation so as to facilitate comprehension.

The knowledge of the audience's self–interest, or *"What's in it for me?,"* is an essential tool for structuring a presentation so it hits the target of the collective mind of audience members.

2.3   Style

This is the most frequently–ignored pillar of the speaking art by substantive experts, possibly because it has the connotation of show business. It refers to word choice, body language, movement and vocal quality.

Style is that almost indefinable quality of a speaker that causes audience members, even those opposed to the issue being sold, to listen, not be bored, and to open their minds. Another word of caution: *Style* without *Substance* can expose the speaker to the charge of being shallow.

Now, let us take a look at the structure supported by these pillars: the *Pyramid* from base to apex, of *Planning, Practicing,* and *Presenting.*

2.4   Planning

Planning is the wide base required of any stable structure and any good presentation. It is the single most important building element of any presentation. Unfortunately, most presentations are done with an *inverted Pyramid* as the model, with the narrow base indicating little planning and practice, thus placing all the weight on the presentation. This *lack of planning* frequently results in poor presentations.

Good business sense dictates that the same effort which goes into the development of a product, policy, or service be devoted to the presentation whose purpose is selling this product, policy, or service. The *planning stage* is where the presenter develops a strategy, a game plan, a frame of reference, and a point of view for the presentation.

An important part of the planning process is gathering *Audience Intelligence* – information about the concerns, problems, attitudes, and expectations of that group of people you are about to face in your presentation.

Because the speaker needs to mesh his or her objective for the presentation with the audience's needs and concerns, the more time spent on strategic planning, the easier will be the actual presentation. Thorough planning lays the groundwork for a successful presentation

If planning is so important, why is it frequently ignored? Perhaps because time is the enemy of all, and there are such demands on our time that few people are ready to literally sit down and think. If they do so, however, they gain maximum advantage from a minimum investment of time.

2.5   Practicing

After you have completed the planning stage, you are now ready to start practicing. This is an orderly means to internalize the presentation. You will take some of the apprehension out of the experience by anticipating reactions, comments and questions and developing appropriate responses.

An important tool in practicing is conducting a *Murder Board*, a realistic simulation of the presentation in front of a suitable audience, e.g. colleagues, relatives, friends, who can put your knowledge to the test. Yet your mistakes won't count because if you fail you can go back to the planning stage and make the necessary corrections.

Your confidence zooms when you have gone through a practice phase that enables you to say: *"I know this subject better than anyone in the audience. I want them to take their best shot, because I'll be able to answer any question thrown at me!"* That is the attitude you want to carry with you to the presentation.

2.6   Presenting

Finally, you reach that apex, the actual presentation. This is the payoff for the time you have spent assuring you have included all the required *substance*, placed within a *structure* that facilitates audience comprehension and agreement with the position you are advocating, done with the *style* most appropriate to make your presentation memorable and successful.

If you have (1) done the planning, to include *audience intelligence* collection, and developed a focus that meshes with audience members' needs and concerns, (2) then practiced with focus, to include an intensive simulation enabling you to anticipate questions and objections, you are ready for "show-time."

Chapter 3

The Ideal Presentation

I don't want to raise false hopes with the title of this chapter. You will probably not learn to make an ideal presentation by reading these pages; I have delivered almost 2,000 presentations, and have yet to make one that meets the description of ideal or perfect.

If I ever did, I would start to worry, because there would be only one direction to go after such a performance. Down.

What I describe in this chapter, based on my experience in speaking and conducting hundreds of presentation skills workshops, are the goals which all who want to become better presenters must keep in mind as they develop their presentations.

3.1 Solve the audience's problems

The fundamental reason people listen to a presentation is to gain information that will solve a problem, fill an informational need, and give them an "edge." As a presenter, you must realize this at the outset. Attempting to impress your audience with your erudition, or with the features of your product or service, will fall on deaf ears if you do not show how this product or service will help audience members.

I will point out over and over again in this book the need to seek focused *intelligence* on the audience members or clients. Acquiring as much information on the audience as possible is absolutely essential for an effective and persuasive presentation. Learn the problems faced by the audience, then construct a presentation that shows how these problems can be solved.

3.2 *Get to the point* early

Because of the overwhelming demands on our time and the multi–tasking we are all involved in, none of us has the patience to listen to a presenter like *Beetle Bailey's* Lt. Fuzz who takes a long time to *get to the point*. Your audience members want an idea of the route you are taking, and the eventual destination.

If the audience is mystified as to where you are taking them in this journey, they will probably tune out early. If you are going to solve problems, let your listeners know up front that you know what these problems are, and let them know you have a solution.

3.3 Give audience members "presentation ammunition"

Keep in mind that everyone must present to someone higher in the corporate food chain. In a sales context, if you are presenting to a person who does not have the power to authorize a purchase, keep that person's boss in mind as you are preparing your presentation.

That means your *intelligence gathering* must operate on more than one level. Without being too obvious, provide the person without the *buying decision power* with ammunition he or she can use when making your case further up the line. You'll be gaining points with this person, as you will be making him or her look smart in front of the boss.

3.4   Provide *maximum* relevant data

For the same reason that you wish to *get to the point early*, you must also avoid doing a "data dump" on your listeners. They only want information which will solve their problems. The more words and facts you present, the greater the likelihood that your essential message will be lost. Short–term memory is precisely that.

As new information is presented, it tends to push the just heard information out, somewhat akin to the *First In, First Out (FIFO)* accounting method.

If, however, the factual information is tied to the needs, wants and concerns of the audience – its problems –audience members will retain the information most relevant to their needs and problems.

Presenting this relevant data in such a way that it will be retained is a function of *structure*. I'll discuss how to develop a tested and proven method to develop this all–important structure of the presentation in Chapter 8.

A word of caution, however. Despite the importance of structuring your information in a logical, coherent manner, structure alone is not enough. A presentation can have superb structure and still fail if it is delivered by a boring presenter.

3.5   Present in *minimum* time

Time limits are generally set by the audience or client, and having a finite time to present is actually a benefit to the presenter. An expert on a given issue or subject, or an enthusiastic sales person, could speak for hours, a recipe for disaster.

Having a time limit, however, forces the presenter to focus on providing that *maximum relevant information* keyed to solving the audience members' problems and needs.

This requires a willingness to edit your own words without mercy. The rigorous practice session described in Chapter 13 – the *Murder Board* – will give you an accurate idea of the length of your actual presentation. It is during and after this practice session when you can pare off minutes. This editing, combined with accurate knowledge of the needs of the audiences, will make your presentation more crisp and *to the point.*

It's best to come in "under budget" on time. You will be considered efficient if you provide the relevant information in less than the time allocated. If, on the other hand, you go over the allotted time, you will be considered inefficient, and you will have stolen audience members' most valuable commodity – their time.

Here's a tip. Have a colleague sit behind the audience, or in the rear of the room, and give you unobtrusive signals when you hit "three minutes left" and "one minute left."

Avoid looking at your watch. Although glancing at your watch demonstrates you are sensitive to the time needs of the audience, it can also cause members of the audience to shift their attention from the substance of your presentation to the question: *"How much longer will this go on?"*

In certain scored situations, such as a proposal for venture capital, or an oral presentation for a government contract, presenters are penalized for going beyond the time limits and could easily lose the capital infusion or contract they are seeking, no matter how superior their product, service or innovative idea.

Need I say any more about staying within your time limit?

3.6   Present in *clearest* terms possible

When we wish to provide the *maximum relevant data* in *minimum time,* there is the temptation to speak rapidly, much like the Federal Express commercial of a few years ago. Nerves can also cause rapid speaking. This becomes especially critical when the information being presented is complex, and the audience needs time to absorb it.

Again, that intense practice session, in front of colleagues and, if possible, a video camera, will enable you to gauge the optimum delivery rate. Too fast can be confusing, too slow can be boring.

Delivery rate is not the only aspect that can lead to an unclear presentation. Excessive use of jargon, especially if the audience contains people who are not familiar with the terminology, is like using a foreign language.

We will continue with the list game in the next chapter, where we'll cover steps necessary to achieve persuasion.

Chapter 4

Six Steps to Persuasion

Most books on public speaking or presentation skills suggest there are four types of presentation, aimed at either

- Informing
- Entertaining
- Motivating and inspiring
- Persuading

I disagree.

I believe the purpose of *all* presentations, especially in the business world, is *persuading*. Even if you are not looking to make a sale, gain a contract or change audience members' minds, you are still attempting to *persuade* them to listen to you, and to accept your information.

The ideas on *persuading audiences* which are introduced in this chapter will reappear throughout this book. The purpose of this chapter is threefold: (1) to organize these ideas into a practical *six–step process*, (2) to give a quick summary of each of these steps, and (3) to refer the reader to later chapters of the book where these steps are discussed in detail. This chapter can be both a fast–track to persuasive presentations and a "road map" leading you to a more detailed treatment in later chapters.

These are the *six steps to persuasion* that I discuss in my training workshops:

1. Develop a concrete objective – Chapters 7, 9, and 10
2. Gain *Audience Intelligence* – Chapter 6
3. Demonstrate passion about your subject – Chapter 18
4. Structure backwards – Chapter 8
5. Conduct a *Murder Board* – Chapters 13 and 14
6. Conduct a *Post–Presentation Analysis* – Chapter 22

Let us look at these steps individually.

4.1   Develop a concrete objective

Your objective is not merely to deliver a good presentation. An oral presentation is the means to a specific end, and that end is what you want the audience to do with your information. If you are vague in your own mind about what action you want the audience to take, you will not have the focus and thematic unity required in an oral presentation.

A written document such as a memo can be poorly written and appear incoherent on first reading, but its obtuseness can finally be pierced on a second or third reading. The oral presentation must be understood immediately. There are no instant replays.

The goal of your presentation is to persuade audience members to buy your product, service, or project, or the information you are providing, because they see it as solving *their* problem.

Once you have decided on your objective, type it, print it, and paste it on your monitor. Refer to this objective as you progress in your draft. It becomes a compass heading to keep you on course. When you find you are going off on a tangent, redirect towards this objective.

Because you must solve the problems of your audience, you must know precisely what these problems are. That leads to the second step which is vital because it gets to the heart of persuasion – knowing your audience's position on the subject, knowing what problems confront audience members, and their attitudes on the issue.

4.2   Gain *Audience Intelligence*

Members of your audience probably have a great deal on their mind, and you are competing with these preoccupations for attention. They have only limited time to listen to you. You must know what are the hot buttons to push, and which hot buttons to avoid touching, lest you distract your audience from the focus of your presentation.

Conduct research on the internet, talk to people who have spoken to this group before, know the idiosyncrasies of key members of the audience.

The more information you have about the concerns, problems and needs of audience members, the better prepared you will be. Techniques to gain this intelligence will be covered in greater detail in Chapter 6.

For now, just keep in mind that persuasive communication takes place at the intersection of your objective and the needs of the audience. If you fail to reach this intersection, concentrating only on what *you* want, you will not persuade.

4.3   Demonstrate passion about your subject

You must have such a belief that your product or service can solve the problems of audience members that you have a sense of obligation to have them accept your message for their own benefit, not yours.

When you have this passion, it will show in your voice, in your gestures, in your facial expression. Even those predisposed to disagree will listen to you, for they know you are sincere, have grasped their problem, and really want to help.

Audience members who sense that a presenter "knows" them are more likely to invest the time and attention to listen to the presentation, and perhaps adopt the point of view being advocated by the presenter.

Passion provides the intensity that cuts through all the distractions and allows the speaker to connect with the audience. Perhaps the best definition of the linkage of factual, verifiable data delivered with verve and passion was made by a 19th Century minister, Lyman Beecher, who defined persuasion as *"Logic on Fire."*

4.4   Structure backwards

From elementary school on, we have been taught to think in a *1−2−3* or *A−B−C* structure. This is logical, but counter−productive for time−sensitive oral presentations. An effective presenter seeking to persuade must adopt a counter−intuitive method: *structuring backwards, not forward.*

Initiate your draft with your concluding phrase, those words that spring from the intelligence you have gained on your audience that you believe will cause audience members to adopt as their own what you have established as your objective in step one.

In my coaching workshops, I refer to this as my *3–1–2 System*, covered in Chapter 8. I consider system the foundation of my entire training program, and of this book.

4.5   Conduct a *Murder Board*

This is a practice session which I bring to my training program from my military background. It is a rigorous practice session in front of an audience role–playing the people to whom you will present.

The *Murder Board* enables you to hone delivery skills, make mistakes when they don't count, anticipate questions and objections, and, of course, develop crisp, precise answers.

Done right, it will build self–confidence, lessen the apprehension of speaking, and result in a more focused and audience–centered presentation. How to conduct such a simulation is the most important element I teach in my workshop, one that does so much to improve speaking skills.

The better you anticipate, the better you respond. The more "heat" you feel in practice, the better prepared you will be to face demanding audience members. Conversely, of course, the less effective you are in anticipating, the less effective you will be in delivering responsive answers to tough questions.

The *Murder Board*, covered in Chapters 13 and 14, is the presenter's equivalent to the actor's dress rehearsal, the *moot court* preparation of lawyers, and the flight simulator that prepares pilots to deal with emergencies.

4.6   Conduct a post–presentation analysis

The previous five steps take place before and during the presentation, while this final step takes place after the presentation has been concluded – *immediately* after. Conducting such an after–action analysis is counter–intuitive, for our instinct after completing a challenging presentation, perhaps one for a lucrative contract, is to breath a sigh of relief. Failure to carry out this immediate post–presentation analysis, however, is to waste a golden opportunity.

You have prepared arduously for your presentation, and you should seek to gain from this experience, not let the lessons vanish in the mists of memory. Conducting an analysis of the presentation immediately will let you apply this hard–earned knowledge to the next presentation.

Can you delay this review until the next day? Absolutely not. The insights gained about your audience and your performance in the intense experience of the presentation will vanish, for short term memory is precisely that. Without a post presentation analysis, you will have to reinvent the presentation wheel the next time you must make a presentation. Why start from scratch when you can bottle the valuable information gained from the just completed presentation?

In the next chapter, we'll look at how to deal with audience members who, in effect, say *"My mind is made up, don't confuse me with facts."*

Chapter 5

Confronting and Creating Cognitive Dissonance

In 1957, social psychologist Leon Festinger wrote what was destined to become a landmark book on how people process information. In *A Theory of Cognitive Dissonance*, Festinger revealed the results of studies he conducted to measure whether people readily changed their mind when presented with new information that contradicted views they held.

Did they analyze the new data, compare it with the information already possessed, and then arrive at a new conclusion through a rational reasoning process? Or did they stubbornly cling to their existing belief, despite the evidence presented to support the new but contradictory information? What he found was surprising and controversial. Thousands of similar studies, however, have shown Festinger's findings to be valid.

5.1 The Festinger experiments

In his experiments, Festinger concluded that the human mind is not comfortable accommodating two contradictory notions simultaneously.

People want a consistent relationship between their values/beliefs and their actions. When this lack of consistency is present – dissonance in Festinger's phrase – people become uncomfortable, and seek to regain the equilibrium between beliefs and actions.

They wish to reduce the dissonance, and – in the case of an audience listening to a presentation at variance with these existing beliefs – they are able to reduce this dissonance by either (1) rejecting the new information, or (2) accepting it and changing their view to one more consistent with the new information.

In Festinger's experiments, he found that when new information is introduced that contradicts existing attitudes, many people, rather than initiating a rational recalculation, will reject the new information. In effect, the mind wants harmony, and does not want dissonance, or disharmony.

5.2 How we handle dissonance

We become comfortable with a judgment, opinion, or belief and are reluctant to accommodate new information that causes us to change our judgment, opinion, or belief. By changing our mind, we are admitting we had not made a wise choice initially, that we had done insufficient research on the matter.

Curiously, in the case of actions that people performed that tend to counter what they thought were their values and beliefs, they sometimes tend to change these beliefs, thereby rationalizing their actions.

In one of Festinger's experiments, he asked participants as to whether cheating on an examination was always wrong, or if there were situations in which cheating was justified.

He then set up a scenario in which participants were asked to take an examination, success in which would prove beneficial for those achieving a certain grade.

A number of those who had voiced strong moral opposition to cheating were in fact observed looking on the papers of classmates and subsequently, when questioned about the morality of cheating on an examination, expressed a more ambiguous position. They were obviously seeking to justify their actions by changing their beliefs.

5.3   How presenters can create cognitive dissonance

For a presenter, cognitive dissonance is a double–edged sword. If members of the audience are being introduced to information at variance with their beliefs, these people are likely to resist accepting the speaker's message.

They will protect their opinions, despite the lucidity of arguments to the contrary. This can make it difficult to reach such people who are intransigent.

The other side of the sword, however, creates an opportunity for the speaker who can show that he or she is a reasonable, open–minded person, whose values, if not opinions, are similar to those in the audience opposed to the position being advocated.

This can create a degree of cognitive dissonance in certain audience members. They may become uncomfortable with the information they brought to the presentation. They like and respect the messenger, and wonder how they can be in disagreement with the point being advocated by a person so similar to them.

The presenter who can create cognitive dissonance does so because he or she realizes that facts alone do not persuade, and such a presenter has learned to appeal to the emotional and psychological side of the audience.

When you are confronted with an audience appearing to have a high degree of cognitive dissonance, let these people save face by having the new information presented in such a manner that they can avoid being forced to admit to themselves and others that they were wrong.

A speaker representing an organization may accept responsibility for not having provided the new information earlier, thus leading audience members to say to *"Had I known that information, I would naturally have come to a different conclusion than I did. Now, with this new data, I will use reason and change my mind."*

In the next chapter, which begins Part II, we'll look at how presenters gain *intelligence* on their audiences.

Part II

Planning

Chapter 6

Audience Intelligence

No, this chapter is not referring to how smart – or not so smart – are the people to whom you are addressing your remarks. Instead, I am referring to the information you need on these people – their needs, concerns, problems, attitudes, expectations, etc. The more you know about audience members, the better you will be able to frame your arguments so they "buy into" what you are proposing.

Another benefit of in–depth knowledge of the audience is that, by definition, it reduces the "fear of the unknown," probably the main driver vaulting *public speaking* to the top of the lists of fears in the United States.

6.1   The need for *Audience Intelligence*

The majority of books on *public speaking* stress the importance of "audience analysis." While I agree wholeheartedly with the concept, as will be demonstrated in this chapter, I vehemently disagree with the term.

You don't *analyze* living, breathing human beings; you acquire the necessary *intelligence* on what they are thinking, what their values are, what their concerns are, what their objections may be to the issue you are addressing. You need this information so you can mesh your objective as speaker with the psychological and informational needs of audience members.

When you can do this, you have a good chance of getting your information into the minds of the audience. Lacking this information causes you to fly blind.

The objective of any speaker must be to "write on the brains" of audience members with his or her ideas in such a way that they adopt the speaker's point of view. This requires, however, that the speaker knows the problems confronting the audience. Below are some thoughts on the nature of audiences, what you need to know about members of the audience, and how you can acquire this information.

6.2   The nature of audiences

The word "audience" causes problems. It is a *collective*, and the unwary may think of that group as a single entity. The reality, of course, is that an audience is composed of individuals. A presentation to fifty people is therefore a presentation to fifty "audiences," as each person will perceive the presentation differently.

Retention of information. The nature of the spoken presentation is that audience members will retain only a small percentage of what they hear. New ideas tend to push out previously heard information. Some estimates are that just a few days after hearing a presentation, only about 10% of the information presented will be retained.

That is one reason why a presentation must have a logical structure that is focused on the needs of the audience, and be delivered with vigor and sincerity. You thus increase the probability your information or proposal will be part of that 10%, not some inane joke used as an "ice breaker."

Self–interest is the prime motivator. It may seem cynical, but the fundamental question audience members have is *"What's in it for me?"* frequently referred to as *WIIFM*. They want to gain some edge from the information you are presenting.

In a sales presentation, your prospective client is making a cost–benefit analysis, weighing the cost of your product or service compared to the potential impact on his or her bottom line.

In order to have the hint of an answer to the *WIIFM* question early in the presentation, the presenter must know the key areas of interest for audience members, especially those in decision–making roles.

Sensitive to time of presentation. Time, as pointed out in Chapter 9, is the most valuable commodity we possess, and audience members want to know how long they will be in the relatively passive role of listeners. If you are expected to speak for ten minutes in a board room, or a sales presentation, you must stay within this limit.

Go beyond ten minutes and you will alienate audience members, who, after all, have other things to do. If, however, you are interrupted with questions during your presentation, few will criticize you for going beyond the stipulated time.

If you know your presentation will last, say, seven minutes, tell the audience this at the outset. They will set their internal clock, and perhaps pay attention more closely because they know they are in a sprint, not a marathon.

6.3   What you need to know about audiences

What are the demographics? A basic area you need to have a handle on is how many people will be in your audience, their age range and educational level. A breakdown by gender and nationality can also be helpful as you frame your presentation.

If there are many women in an audience, severely limit sports and war metaphors. If there are many foreigners in the audience, be careful with your delivery rate, colloquialisms and humor.

What are the needs, wants, concerns, problems of the audience? This is the key to your *Audience Intelligence gathering.* Think of your presentation as the solution being presented to solve the problems of audience members. You must, of course, know what these problems are so you can seek to match them with a solution.

How much do audience members know about the issue? It is imperative that you not waste an audience's time with details already known to these people. You want your presentation to add to the net knowledge they possess. At the same time, you do not want to assume audience members know as much about the subject as you do. After all, you are the expert.

Threading your way between these two extremes, while difficult, is required for those wishing to deliver what the audience considers a successful presentation. The best way is to aim slightly above the level of knowledge you believe the audience has on the subject. Better to have them reach than for them to think you are talking down to them.

Do audience members expect a general overview or a detailed presentation? Another important element of *audience intelligence* is determining audience expectations. Are they expecting an overview of the issue, with follow–up detail to be provided in written material, or is this a "roll up the sleeves, give us all the information you have" group?

Are audience members open–minded or opinionated? Few people are completely open–minded, as they have points of view on the issue. Their self–interest, however, will cause them to shift positions if your presentation shows the benefits that will accrue to them if they adopt your view.

Those who are strongly opposed to what you are "selling" will be a tougher nut to crack, but you must learn what is driving them to take such a strong position. As pointed out in Chapters 24 and 25, you may be able to find some common ground and eventually bring them around.

Who makes the decisions, and who influences him or her? In most business or government presentations, the decision–maker will be the ranking person. This person should, of course, be the target of your presentation. You should also learn before the presentation who this person leans on for advice. A phone call or meeting with this person could facilitate having that advice support your position.

Are there any troublemakers in the audience? There are some people who delight in showing off their knowledge by harassing the presenter. Find out who these people are before the presentation, stroke their delicate egos by asking for their input ahead of time, then mention them during your presentation. They will be less likely to cause trouble.

Are there any audience idiosyncrasies and "hot buttons?" Most of us have some strange quirks, things that turn us on or off. Find out what these are before the presentation. Perhaps the decision–maker dislikes *PowerPoint* presentations. Perhaps he or she delights in interrupting the presentation with questions.

Perhaps there is an issue, internal or external, that while not directly related to the issue you are presenting, could come up. Seek to avoid having it surface if it could distract the audience members, particularly the decision–makers, from focusing on your presentation.

It is better to know any idiosyncrasies before the presentation so adjustments can be made. Practice the presentation with biases of audience members in mind, especially when you are engaged in the *Murder Board* simulation covered in Chapters 13 and 14.

6.4   Means to acquire *Audience Intelligence*

The internet in general, and search engines in particular, are excellent sources of information. The internet has made the collection of *audience intelligence* much easier. Companies have web–sites which can provide specific information on corporate culture, ongoing projects, key personnel etc. Newspapers such as the *Wall Street Journal* have excellent archives on the internet for detailed searches.

Search engines, particularly http://www.google.com, are a treasure trove of intelligence on individuals and organizations. If a person has been mentioned in a trade magazine or other publication, merely type in his or her name and up pops the article.

Newspapers and magazines. Sometimes referred to as the "university of the street," newspapers and magazines (such as *The New York Times, Wall Street Journal, Time, Newsweek,* etc.) can provide timely information on individuals, organizations and current events. Unless you have a clipping service, however, you can become overwhelmed.

LexisNexis. In the interest of full disclosure, as they say on television, I should state here that I have done considerable coaching/training of LexisNexis sales personnel, and I have great admiration for the company.

If you are fortunate to work for a corporation or organization that has an account with LexisNexis, use it to the hilt. It is the equivalent of having the CIA in your employ.

When I was speaking for the State Department, searches on Nexis, as it was called in those pre–merger days, provided me with information about people I was about to debate and their writings, leveling the playing field by showing me the probable game plan they would follow. Forewarned was forearmed.

There are other companies that provide similar services, of course, but in my judgment, LexisNexis simply has no peer when it comes to providing intelligence on virtually any subject you should need for presentations.

People who have presented to this audience. When you are preparing for a presentation, seek out colleagues or others who have presented to this group, or a similar group. Pick their brains for information on how members of this audience reacted, the type of questions they asked, their general attitude etc.

Ask these people to be on your *Murder Board*, (Chapters 13 and 14), the forum where you will initially put all the intelligence you have gained to use.

6.5   Some final words on *Audience Intelligence*

Successful, persuasive presenters are audience–centered, not speaker–centered. They show an interest in solving the problems of the audience. To do so requires insight into precisely what those problems are.

Rarely will you have all of the information you crave on an audience's problems. If you follow the advice in this chapter, however, you'll have far more insight on the needs and problems of audience members than most presenters ever have on the people to whom they are speaking.

Keep in mind that *audience intelligence* collection is a process. It starts when you know you are going to speak to this particular audience. The process continues during your presentation. You "read" the audience and assess how your information is being received. If necessary you change pace, add new information, delete something you planned to say based on this ongoing analysis.

As stated at the beginning of this chapter, the fundamental reason why speaking to groups is so feared in the United States is *fear of the unknown*. Acquiring needed information about the audience will do much to reduce the unknown, and you'll enter the presentation in control of the data as well as your emotions.

In the next chapter, we'll see how lawyers, who certainly must *collect intelligence* before they enter the courtroom, structure their presentations so they will have maximum impact on juries, a lesson presenters can carry into the boardroom and sales presentation.

Chapter 7

Courtroom Lessons: *Primacy* and *Recency*

The *Doctrine of Primacy and Recency* has long been a staple of trial lawyers, and it can be equally beneficial to presenters who wish to organize their presentations with clarity and coherence.

Simply stated, it is based on the empirical evidence that people – audiences, clients, juries – tend to remember what they hear at the beginning and end of a presentation. Various studies suggest that all the factual data in between is not remembered in any systematic detail.

7.1 How juries remember conflicting arguments

Trial lawyers realize that juries, overloaded with technical, conflicting information, will best remember what they hear first (primacy) and last (recency). Thus the great attention paid to *opening statements* and *closing arguments*.

Most trial lawyers consider them the most important part of their courtroom procedures. Many will start their actual trial preparation with a draft *closing argument*, then go immediately to a draft *opening statement.*

Working backward, they can see what evidence needs to be emphasized at the beginning of the trial so it can be re–emphasized in the *closing argument* to provide the most persuasive "punch."

Following this backward planning approach enables them to see more clearly both the strong and weak points of their argument, and of course, to anticipate the counter–arguments of their adversaries. Developing their oral arguments with the *closing argument* in mind is like having a road map showing how to get to a particular destination.

Shortly after the conclusion of the O. J. Simpson trial in 1995, a noted trial lawyer was on a television program strongly criticizing the prosecution team of the Los Angeles District Attorney's office.

He said he had learned that Marcia Clark, the lead prosecutor, had started preparing her *closing argument* the night before she delivered it. The non–lawyer host asked: *"Well, when she should she have started preparing it?"* The lawyer exploded: *"Before the trial began."*

7.2 *Primacy* and *Recency* for presenters

My first exposure to the recency–primacy theory had come a few years earlier. I had written an essay, *The Art of Making Winning Presentations,* and had sent it to an old Army friend who was by then a successful trial lawyer.

He called me a few days later, asking for permission to make copies to distribute to other lawyers in his firm, as he said the essay contained excellent advice for those engaged in litigation.

He added that it was clear to him that I was a *Primacist*. Knowing I didn't have the slightest idea what he meant, he explained the primacy and recency concept. He went on to tell me that there were strong differences of opinion among legal scholars on whether *opening statements* or *closing arguments* were more important, and law journals were replete with learned articles on the subject.

Many, if not most, presenters start their presentation weakly, perhaps with a joke, and end with a *"Well, that's about it."* They put their emphasis on the detailed "meat" of the presentation but give short shrift to the beginning and end.

But primacy and recency are just as important for a presenter as they are for a trial lawyer. Audiences and juries alike can remember what they hear first and last, but may not recall much of what they hear in between.

If you do not grab the audience's attention with a strong opening, a dynamite close will have less impact because the audience may not have been inspired to listen to the factual data leading up to the conclusion. They may also lack the context of your presentation.

The overriding advantage of applying the primacy and recency concept to making of presentations is that it helps develop both focus and thematic unity. If you first develop your *conclusion* – the equivalent of the lawyer's *closing argument* – then you know how the presentation will turn out .

A presenter must always accommodate the information to be presented to the time to be allocated for the presentation. By initially developing your *Bottom Line Conclusion*, you can build backwards in a time–efficient manner. Doing so also provides you with a mini-presentation if the time allocated is suddenly reduced. This will be covered in the next chapter where the *3–1–2 System* will be introduced.

Chapter 8

Easy as *3–1–2*: Structuring Backwards

An area I am frequently asked to address when brought into companies to help executives to become better presenters is their lack of focus, clarity and their ability to *get to the point.* Solving this problem requires only counter–intuitive thinking, a stack of 3x5 cards, and my *structuring backwards 3–1–2 System.*

What are the benefits of this system? *Backward Planning* makes it less likely that you will go off on an audience–confusing tangent. You will be able to structure your presentation so the audience members know where you are taking them.

The *3–1–2 System* is analogous to the flight plan a pilot files before taking off, as I will illustrate later with a true story of one of my former students.

8.1   The last minute schedule change

Let's set the stage for explaining how this system can help you by way of an imaginary scenario. Let's say you have been tasked to make an important presentation to your boss, or a board of directors, or perhaps an important client.

You are told you will have twenty minutes to make your case. You prepare in the traditional way, which I'll call the *1–2–3 System* of *Opening, Body*, and *Conclusion.*

You practice diligently, develop excellent visuals, and have edited your presentation to just under twenty minutes. Comes the big day, and you show up a the appropriate location on time, only to be told that, because of extenuating circumstances, schedule conflicts, unforeseen delays etc., you will have only about one minute to make your presentation. Now the pressure is on you to make a dramatic adjustment. You have a few options:

First, you can say: *"Sorry, my information simply cannot be done in one minute. Call me when they have the time to listen to the entire presentation."* This may not be a career–enhancing option.

Second, you can try to speak as fast as the famous Federal Express spokesperson of television fame, enabling you to get maximum information into that minimum time allotted you, but your audience will probably think you are a blabbering idiot.

Third, as you are approaching the audience – be it one person or a group – you desperately try to think of the most important part of your presentation. It's not likely you will be able to do so, because you have prepared from the front, not the back.

You are not alone. Most people prepare their presentations using a *1–2–3 Method* – drafting in the order of how they will deliver – (1) Opening, (2) Body and (3) Conclusion. This is the method to organize our thoughts we have been taught since elementary school.

Unfortunately, this system leads to various false starts, because the presenter is attempting to place the ten gallons of knowledge he or she possesses on the subject into the eight–ounce glass of the presentation. It is definitely not flexible, and forces the presenter to make changes on the fly. This may result in time–pressed presentations lacking coherence. In effect, the traditional system of organizing our thoughts is simply not geared to presentations in the 21st century.

8.2   The *3–1–2 System*

Presentations today must, as pointed out earlier, get to the point, focus on the needs of the audience, and be easily understood by audience members. These tasks are the responsibility of the presenter.

Time is the defining aspect of any presentation. Few audiences have the time for a full exposition of a subject. The presenter must reduce and translate the salient data into an easily and quickly understood message. The *3–1–2 System* enables presenters to organize their thoughts in the optimum manner to implant their message in the collective mind of the audience.

Let's wake up from that nightmare scenario described above, which, of course, is the way things generally work. If you had prepared your presentation with the *3–1–2 System* I'll describe here, you would have been unflustered when asked to reduce your twenty minute presentation to one minute – you would have already done so in your planning and practicing stages.

Using this system will enable you to present voluminous content within the limited amount of time your audience may have to listen to you. You'll have more focus, because you will know when you start drafting where you are going in the presentation. Most importantly, your audience will see a structure to your presentation enabling them to follow and, in the best of cases, ultimately agree with your argument.

The *3–1–2 System* is counter–intuitive, but it results in a more focused presentation that can easily be adjusted. Here are some steps to aid you in getting off on the right foot in preparing any presentation.

1. Place a *30–60 second Bottom Line* of your message on a 3x5 card. You have gained *intelligence* on the audience needs and problems, you have a specific objective. The phrase which you believe will result in the intersection of the audience's needs and your objective goes on this card, which you mark with a (3).

2. Place in front of this phrase words that signal the close of your presentation, such as: *"So, in conclusion"* or *"Let me leave you with this thought."* You now have the words with which you will get off stage. This is your *closing argument*. It can also provide you with a *mini–presentation* when you face that last minute and dramatic reduction of time for your presentation noted above.

3. Take another 3x5 card, mark it with a (1) and write an opening phrase that will motivate the audience to listen to you because you have hit a psychological "hot button" that sends the signal to the audience: *"This will benefit you,"* or *"This will keep you out of trouble."* A startling statistic or an apt quotation from a well–known (to the audience) figure could also be in this beginning as an attention–getter.

65

4. An effective technique is to include your (3) card conclusion in a your *opening statement*, and then inform the audience that you will now proceed to prove the validity of your conclusion.

5. The audience now knows where you are going, and can, in effect, open the "files" on their mental desktops to absorb this information. Remember that a business presentation is not a mystery novel. You want your audience to know "who shot John" right away, and then show the evidence. Above all, you want your audience to be alerted to the fact that you know what their material or psychological needs/problems are, and are prepared to provide information that addresses these concerns.

6. With the (3) and (1) cards filled out, you have the parameters of your presentation established, and this will help you in the drafting stage as you develop the body of your presentation in (2). Most importantly, you will avoid going off on a tangent or confuse your audience with too much detail.

7. You know where you are going, and can thus structure your presentation so the audience can know where you are taking them. Take a few cards, marked (2A), (2B), (2C), etc. and list your supporting arguments.

The *3−1−2 System* ensures that the most important information you wish the audience to retain and act upon is placed at the *beginning* and the *end*. Whether you are a believer in *Primacy* or *Recency* as the best way of implanting information in the collective mind of an audience, the *3−1−2 System* is an improvement on the traditional 1−2−3 system of drafting that you have probably used most of your lives.

8.3 The *3–1–2 System* and the F–14 Pilot

Let me conclude this chapter with a story from my training workshops. A few years ago, I was conducting such a program for the U.S. Navy. There were ten participants – Naval officers and Department of the Navy civilians.

As I was explaining my *3–1–2 System*, all the participants, save one, were nodding in agreement, seeing the logic and the benefits of this new system The exception was a young Naval aviator. As I explained, he rolled his eyes and shook his head, obviously not buying. I said: *"Lieutenant, I don't think we're on the same page. What is it you don't like?"*

He responded that he did not see how one could start with a conclusion until the thesis had been posited, and then the evidence would lead to the conclusion.

I recognized him as a linear thinker whose vocabulary would never include the phrase *"Thinking outside the box."* I then learned he was an Annapolis graduate, had an MS in aeronautical engineering, and was an F–14 Tomcat pilot – all indications of a very intelligent person.

He was locked into his conventional 1–2–3 linear thinking, and, despite my efforts, he could not accept my *3–1–2 System*. Then I hit upon a way to reach him. He was assigned to a Pentagon desk job, a position anathema to fighter pilots.

I asked him if he would volunteer to ferry an F–14 from Andrews Air Force base outside Washington to Pensacola Naval Air Station in Florida. His reply, as I recall, was *"in a New York minute."* I then proceeded to ask him what he would do before taking off. He replied he would file a flight plan, which would include altitude and heading of his flight.

I asked him what would determine the heading, or direction, of his flight, and how he would know how much fuel to would carry, or whether he would require mid–air refueling. He initially had a puzzled look on his face, wondering about my curious questions.

Then, he smiled and said, *"That would be determined by my destination. So you are telling me that the (3) in your system is the same as where I'm going to put wheels down."*

He turned out to be an excellent presenter, with focused, to the point presentations. A few months later I was visiting the Pentagon to have lunch with a friend, and the Lieutenant, now promoted to Lieutenant Commander, saw me. He thanked me, saying whenever he had to brief the Secretary of the Navy, he planned his briefing along the lines of a flight plan. He added he was now an ardent believer in the *3–1–2 System.*

One of the principal benefits of organizing with the *3–1–2 System* will be discussed in the next chapter: Should you ever find yourself in a situation where a last–minute schedule change drastically reduces the amount of time you have available for your presentation, the *3–1–2 System* will ensure you are well prepared to make the most of your allocated time when you must go to *Plan B,* which we will address in the next chapter.

Chapter 9

The *Plan B* Presentation

In a perfect world, presenters would have the time to deliver their presentation in its entirety. In the real world of the 21st century, however, it is more the rule than the exception that time will be dramatically reduced from that originally allocated for a presentation.

9.1   Presentations and time

A challenge that confronts all presenters, therefore, is time. Audiences may originally have time for a full–blown presentation, then those minutes could be reduced at the last minute. Yet the presenter still has the obligation to provide the information required by the audience.

Question: How can such last–minute schedule changes to presentations be accommodated?

Answer: Have a *Plan B*, a reduced version of your presentation, ready when you walk into the room. You do not want to be in the position of frantically revising your notes and visuals while your audience watches. The old Boy Scout motto *"Be Prepared"* will serve you well.

Generally, the later in the day a presentation is scheduled, the higher the probability is that the time for the presentation will be severely reduced. You may get apologies for putting you in such a position. Nevertheless, it is your responsibility to provide *maximum* information, in *minimum* time, and in the *clearest* manner possible, no matter the circumstances under which you must make the presentation.

This means that you must plan for the very real possibility that you will have less time than you thought you would. Thus the need for the *Plan B* presentation.

9.2 How to develop the *Plan B* presentation

To clarify terms, let's consider your *Plan A* presentation as the one you are planning to deliver within the time limits you have been told you will have. The *Plan B* presentation is the one you may have to deliver within last minute time constraints.

A benefit of the *3–1–2 System* discussed in the last chapter is that by definition, a presentation thus developed is not a "stream of consciousness seamless whole," but instead one that is composed of connected, but at the same time independent, modules.

This method creates a presentation that is elastic, in that it can be expanded or contracted. There are required components, (1) the *Opening* and (3) the *Conclusion*, and several optional components in (2) – the *Body*.

Constructing your presentation with the *3–1–2 System* facilitates adjusting to last minute changes in the schedule that result in having your allotted time reduced. The components of the 3–1–2 planning and drafting process – (3) Conclusion – (1) Opening – (2) Body – allow you to build the *Plan A* and the *Plan B* presentations simultaneously. The result is a presentation that can be expanded, or more likely, contracted, easily.

9.3 The modular method: Key to *Plan B* presentations

Let's look at how you can go the *Plan A* and *Plan B* routes in developing your presentation with the 3–1–2 System. The key is thinking of your presentation as a series of modules.

The need for cards. To ensure maximum flexibility, cards, preferably 3x5 but larger are acceptable if desired, must be the medium used. To have a presentation on paper such as 8.5x11 sheets will make deleting/adding the optional elements too cumbersome.

The cards should be marked to show their priority. I use a red felt tip pen to show absolutely needed, green for very useful and blue for nice to have.

Write in large letters, and put a sequential numbering system on the cards. Your objective must be to find the cards quickly so you can organize your "new" presentation rapidly. Additionally, having the cards numbered will help you get back on track if they fall to the floor.

The (3) and (1) foundation. The (3) card, as we discussed in the last chapter, is the *Bottom Line*, the words which will answer the fundamental question of all audiences: *"What's in it for me?"*

The (1) card contains the opening that causes audience members to listen, and to conclude immediately that their problem can be solved by this presentation. It is this *Return On Investment (ROI)* opening which provokes audience members to pay attention because of self–interest.

There should be such a logical connection between the (1) and (3) cards that when time is dramatically reduced, perhaps to one minute or less, these two statements can comprise the entire presentation. It is *Maximum information in minimum time in the clearest form possible.*

All presentations, consequently, require the (3) and (1) components, although in extreme cases there could be such a time constraint that only the *Bottom Line Conclusion*, or (3), is articulated.

The optional elements. The elasticity and flexibility of the presentation is provided by a series of cards, marked (2A), (2B), (2C), etc. that contain the supporting evidence, the information that connects the Opening (1) and Conclusion (3).

In developing these supporting points, make them self–sufficient. You do not want one card to be dependent for understanding on a preceding or following card. Such cards become the modules to be added or deleted as time permits.

So long as the (1) and (3) cards are included, the minimum information required by the audience is provided. As the time is increased, cards/modules can be added.

The *Plan B* contingency. Now we come to the *Plan B* contingency. When you are developing your main supporting points, the various (2) cards – (2A), (2B), (2C), etc. provide the logical scaffolding for the presentation.

For maximum flexibility, organize your presentation so that the various (2) cards have their own supporting evidence – *nice to know* but not *need to know*.

For example, you will have a card marked (2A), a principal supporting pillar of your presentation, which is in turn supported by cards marked (2A i), (2A ii), (2A iii), etc. Do the same with the 2B and 2C cards.

Dividing your supporting evidence into these sub–categories will enable you to reduce your presentation as time demands. You can delete the (i), (ii), and (iii) cards if you do not have the time for the full presentation. Although reduced, the presentation maintains its internal consistency and coherence.

Visuals. A factor complicating the rapid shift to the *Plan B* presentation is the visual support medium you are using. It is easier if you are using overhead transparencies, because you can mark the cardboard frames to show relative importance, and merely use the most salient overheads.

With *PowerPoint*, one solution is to have separate disks for your original, full length presentation, and the *Plan B* presentation. Just substitute one for the other, and you are good to go.

Alternatively, you can have a paper or card next to the projector listing the number of each of the *Plan B* slides. When presenting, just hit the number of the slide and the return button, and *PowerPoint* will show only those slides which are pertinent to the *Plan B* presentation.

If you are using 35mm slides, the best alternative is to have a separate carousel containing the reduced slide show.

9.4 How *Plan B* can help you

The obvious benefit of developing a contingency plan for a reduced presentation is to provide your audience members with information they require, despite the reduced time.

There is an added benefit for the presenter who delivers an excellent presentation under such difficult circumstances. If you can appear to be unflustered by the changed situation, and move effortlessly into the reduced time, you will appear as a person who has his or her act together, a skill that will transcend the presentation itself.

You will appear organized and professional. It will demonstrate to, say, superiors in your organization or company, that you can operate under pressure and have the ability to think ahead – a highly valued trait. So having your time reduced may not be such a bad thing to happen after all.

In the next chapter, we'll cover how to draft your presentation for the ear, not write an essay for the eye.

Chapter 10

For the Ear, not the Eye

Because words are the vehicles by which we transmit our thoughts to others, and because we receive more formal training in writing than speaking, there is an understandable tendency to draft a presentation as if we are writing a memo or essay.

The emphasis from grade school to college is on the written, not the spoken, word. Speaking is considered a natural process, but writing well is a discipline replete with rules and conventions.

Far more emphasis is placed in our years of formal education on strengthening our written communication skills. We certainly cannot write as automatically as we can speak.

We start to communicate and persuade orally as soon as we leave our mother's womb, but we only start to learn how to express our thought in writing in the first grade.

As a result of so much training in writing and so little in speaking, we frequently fall back on the lessons learned about writing when we are called on to make a spoken presentation. That is a mistake.

10.1 How writing and speaking differ

Because of this emphasis in writing over speaking, we must always be alert that the two disciplines contain significant differences. In effect, to be a good speaker, you have to "unlearn" many of the rules and conventions about writing so that you do not deliver an oral essay that may look good to the eye on paper, but may not sound good to the ear when heard by your audience.

It is how audience members hear you that determines how they will accept your message. Whenever preparing an oral presentation, your target is the ear, not the eye.

10.2 A history lesson

When Ted Sorenson, President John F. Kennedy's speechwriter, finished the first draft of a speech the President was to deliver, he would come to the Oval Office and read it to JFK.

The President wanted to hear how the phrases sounded to the ear, just as his audiences would hear his speech. Follow Kennedy's lesson and, after you have drafted your presentation, read it into a tape recorder, then listen. Do you sound natural and conversational, or stilted and excessively formal? If you cringe at how you sound, work on your inflection, on your pacing, on eliminating, or at least reducing, the *"uh's"* and *"y'knows"* that plague so many speakers.

The remainder of this chapter contains tips to help you make your presentation play better to the ear, even if on paper it does not look as good the eye as a well crafted essay.

10.3   Options for drafting the presentation

The most tedious part of preparing a presentation is certainly the drafting stage. It brings to mind the writer's lament *"I love having written, but I hate writing."* There are three approaches to take in drafting a presentation, and they can be combined.

Verbatim: Writing your presentation out as an essay has the advantage of assuring that most of the key points will be covered. The fundamental disadvantage to this practice is that you will use words and syntax more appropriate for the written medium, and not the more conversational style of the oral presentation.

Other disadvantages of the verbatim draft are: (1) If taken to the lectern, it becomes a crutch. This may cause the speaker to (2) read the presentation, and that in turn will result in (3) falling back to our habit to speak in a mind–numbing monotone and at the much faster silent reading speed.

Outline: The outline is the form we are normally most comfortable with, but we can find that logical fallacies can creep into the presentation, and key points may be omitted.

But it is time–saving, and has the advantage of drafting in the more cryptic manner which we speak and the audience listens.

"Memory joggers:" Placing key points on 3x5 cards is an excellent time–saving device when you are in full command of the data. The disadvantage is that you may omit key points "in the heat of battle," or even when you are in the drafting stage.

Combining all three of these methods is best if you have the time: Write out the initial draft verbatim, then reduce it to an outline, and finally place the key points of the outline on 3x5 cards.

Going through this procedure, because of repetition, has the added benefit of allowing you to internalize the data more readily, and you will find you will make only minimum use of even your "memory joggers" when you are actually delivering the presentation.

You'll also find that your self–confidence in speaking to a group increases dramatically as you become more assured of your command of the data.

10.4　Tricks of the drafting trade

Use contractions. When we write, we have been schooled to put on paper phrases such as "We do not..." If we use this rule when making a presentation, the tendency will be to sound somewhat stuffy.

It is better in a presentation to say "We don't..." for that is how we would probably express the thought in a conversation. Speaking today is actually a conversation writ large, not an erudite dissertation.

Even presidents of the United States avoid the written style when making a speech, no matter how weighty the issue. These leaders recognize the need for a conversational tone to connect with the American people.

Use short, even one–sentence, paragraphs. When you took writing courses in high school and college, a red pencil was probably applied generously by the teacher or professor to a paper with one-sentence paragraphs. Complete thoughts were normally considered needing more than one sentence. But in a spoken presentation, a one–sentence paragraph adds punch to your thoughts.

Be repetitive. In writing, economy of words is a principle, and excessive repetition would draw the ire and red pencil of that same teacher. In speaking, however, repetition of key thoughts and ideas is necessary, for audiences tune in and tune out.

In a written document, a reader, when distracted or sleepy, can put down the paper, and then pick it up later. In the oral presentation, there is no instant replay, so the speaker, aware of the likelihood that listeners will drift off, must repeat the key points, using slightly different phrases to express the same point.

When the muse strikes, use your cell phone. Once you start the drafting process, you'll find the creative juices flow at unexpected moments. Let's say you are driving in congested traffic when a brilliant idea for your presentation comes to you. How can you capture this attack from the right brain?

You can't write it down if you are driving, and you may not have a tape recorder handy. If it is permitted in your state to use a cell phone while driving, and if you can do so safely, then place a call to your answering machine. Your spontaneous brilliance has been captured for posterity, and for you to include in your presentation.

I can't count the number of times I have done this, even walking down the street. No one thinks you are weird, because everybody else is talking into their cell phones.

Use simple language. The audience of a spoken presentation will not have access to a dictionary, so try to not impress these people with your vocabulary. When an audience member is trying to remember what a particular word means, he or she will be missing what you are saying next.

Sir Winston Churchill, certainly one of the great speakers of the 20th century, was an advocate of the simple word and the short sentence. His speeches are masterpieces of communication.

Come back to this chapter when you get to Chapter 19, which addresses what to do when you must read a presentation to an audience.

Part III

Practicing

Chapter 11

The Need to Anticipate: A Case History

You probably remember an exchange between two political candidates which was witnessed by millions of Americans It took place in October 1988.

> **Senator Lloyd Bentsen:** *"I knew Jack Kennedy. Jack Kennedy was a friend of mine. Senator, you are no Jack Kennedy."*

> **Senator Dan Quayle**: *"That was uncalled for."*

The remark by Bentsen, and Quayle's stunned reaction, was perhaps the most devastating and best–remembered exchange in the history of American political debates. Dan Quayle's image was permanently damaged, even though the Bush–Quayle ticket went on to win the November 1988 election.

11.1 Lessons from the 1988 debate

The Bentsen–Quayle debate provides an excellent lesson for business presenters. You must always anticipate the most daunting objection and the most difficult question from your audience. Failure to do so could result in public humiliation, the fate suffered by then–Senator Quayle. Although you may never be in public debate, you will probably face demanding audiences. Be ready for their questions and objections, and develop your responses and rebuttals.

Despite the fact that Quayle was, by all accounts, an effective Vice President, he never recovered from the Bentsen broadside. His every gaffe of the next four years was exaggerated by the media and TV comedians because it fit the image of the youthful, bumbling, politician first established in the debate.

The lingering effects of 1988 may have had an impact on the 1992 elections as well, as Democratic Vice Presidential candidate Al Gore was generally perceived as more "presidential," despite the fact that Quayle had been the proverbial heartbeat from the presidency for four years.

11.2 The lost opportunity

Ironically, it did not have to be that way. In his memoirs, Quayle acknowledges that he and his advisers anticipated that Bentsen might make an unfavorable comparison of him to President Kennedy.

The Republicans had started the comparison game, seeking to bolster Quayle's image by pointing out that he was about the same age that Kennedy was in 1960, and that each man had served approximately the same number of years in Congress.

Having done a good job of anticipating the Kennedy comparison, Quayle's advisers made a colossal blunder in advising him not to mention Kennedy, perhaps naively believing Bentsen would not initiate the comparison without provocation.

In the rhetorical combat that public debate has become, wishful thinking has no place in the planning process – the worst–case scenario must be the guiding principle.

Those preparing Quayle for the debate failed to develop a counter–attack to a punch they saw coming. Although it is impossible to anticipate all the lines of attack of an adversary, it is inexcusable to fail to develop a rebuttal to an all–but–certain hit.

Bentsen's invidious comparison of Quayle to Kennedy was indeed predictable. In 1988, Quayle's selection as George Bush's running mate had been widely criticized, due to the Senator's relative youth. To lessen the impact, Republican spin–masters repeatedly drew those age and experience–related comparisons to Kennedy.

The Democrats were upset at this seizing of a Democratic icon, and, as the date of the debate drew near, probably set out to recapture JFK for their own, at the expense of Quayle.

11.3 How history could have been changed

Could Quayle have anticipated Bentsen's attack? Why did his "handlers," as he derisively described them, not develop in advance a response to turn the tables on Bentsen and his obvious attack line by providing Quayle with another comparison – that of Kennedy to the man at the top of the 1988 Democratic ticket, Governor Michael Dukakis?

Think how effective this response to Bentsen would have been, had Quayle and his advisers only decided to act on their worst fears, rather than put their heads in the sand and hope for the best:

> *"Senator Bentsen, if you want to say who is not a John F. Kennedy, let me point out that your running mate, the ultra–Liberal Michael Dukakis, is a far cry from the tough–minded Jack Kennedy. The only thing they have in common is the state of Massachusetts."*

Such a response would have taken little imagination to devise. Quayle and his advisers could have even turned a lemon into lemonade by luring Bentsen into an "ambush," as a means of guaranteeing the hit on Dukakis.

Quayle's risk–aversive coaches took the cautious approach, hoping Bentsen would avoid the very attack they saw coming. Quayle and the Republican Party were ill–served by such incompetence.

Had Quayle delivered such a response, his supporters in the audience would have responded with robust applause, Bentsen's comment would not have captured the headlines (and history), and Quayle would have been credited with a quick–thinking comeback.

The exchange would probably have been forgotten, and Quayle, who did well in the rest of the debate, would have possibly been viewed as the winner, or at worst the debate would have been judged a draw. Instead, he was considered the clear loser.

The failure to prepare for Bentsen's obvious JFK comparison had a profound impact on Dan Quayle's political career.

11.4 The need to think ahead

The lesson business presenters can draw from Quayle's unfortunate experience is to always anticipate the worst case scenario unfolding, and develop plans to at least lessen the damage.

When faced with a skeptical audience, speakers must keep in mind that the information they are presenting is not going into empty vessels, but is mixing with the biases of audience members. These people will not give up their preconceived opinions without a fight.

Consequently, anticipating how audience members will react, and what lines of attack they may take against the position you are advocating, is an absolute necessity for the person preparing to speak to an audience *with its mind made up.*

You may feel confident in your ability to think fast, but it is invariably better to follow a systematic methodology that hones the ability to anticipate audience reactions and develop responses based on this intelligence.

The next three chapters spell out in detail a proven practice method to make mistakes when they don't count, learn from these miscues, and then deliver a dazzling presentation.

Chapter 12

Practicing Smart:
Solo and with a Colleague

Now that you have a draft – preferably in outline or notes form – you are ready to hear the sound of your voice. Don't think you can practice by sitting at your desk and reading silently or in a low tone.

You must speak at the volume you will use in the actual presentation. Among the worst mistakes presenters make is to have silent practice. They then hear their voice for the first time when delivering these words in front of their real audience, and this can be distracting.

In addition to unlimbering the vocal chords, practicing aloud has another advantage; reinforcement of the concepts you are now attempting to internalize for an extemporaneous presentation.

By hearing yourself speak, the words become more ingrained in your mind. It's like hearing a song – the more you listen, the more you remember the words. Think of practicing as building houses of information in your mind.

12.1 Practicing solo

Do this initial practicing without another person present. You will be at your weakest initially as you go from notes to delivering a crisp, extemporaneous presentation. You do not want anyone present during these sessions because your confidence could be irreparably damaged by comments this person may make.

Wait until you have gained more control over the data and your delivery, have reduced your "uh's" and "y'knows" and are ready for exposure to a friendly critic.

After finishing your draft, using the *3−1−2 System*, speak it aloud in front of a mirror, or even better a video camera and with a tape recorder (see below) so you become familiar with how you look and sound. Pay careful attention to your facial expression.

When appropriate, smile. When delivering somber news, make sure you have a somber look on your face. Audiences will note any inconsistency between content and non−verbal signals.

Note especially if you are saying "uh" or "y'know", and if you are speaking in a monotone. Listen as well for the rate of delivery. A comfortable rate is about 150 words per minute.

A bit faster can connote enthusiasm, which is good, but a consistent "machine−gun" delivery can overwhelm an audience, and your pearls of wisdom will not be comprehended by the audience. Speaking too slowly could put your audience to sleep

Concentrate on removing the "uh's" and "you knows" by substituting a pause. If you are speaking in a monotone, use a highlighter or pen to underline on your notes those words that demand inflection, such as "excited," "generated."

12.2 The importance of an audio– and/or video–camera

Recording your solo practice by means of a tape recorder and/or a video camera will allow you to see and hear yourself as your audience will see and hear you. A word of caution; Don't purchase a micro–cassette audio–recorder, the ones that look like a TV remote. The tapes are small, can easily be misplaced, and the sound quality is horrible.

Use instead the small, hand–held recorder that takes a standard size audio tape. After recording your practice sessions, listen on a good tape deck so you can determine your vocal quality.

Alternatively, most of today's PCs are capable of producing digital recordings. You only need to connect an external microphone to the appropriate jack and start your recording software. Provided your sound–card and speakers are good enough, this can be a very versatile tool for analyzing your presentation.

During your solo practice, place the tape recorder about 15 feet from you. This will approximate the human ear listening capability. If you must then turn the volume to maximum to hear yourself during playback, you are not speaking with sufficient volume.

The same advice applies for a video camera, which you will want to use for close–ups at least one time in order to judge facial expression, and a longer view to judge your body language and any disturbing mannerisms you may have.

When viewing the video tape, watch for your gestures and facial expressions, as well as listening to the tone and inflection of your voice. Do some close–ups to check your facial expression. Always keep in mind that the person you see on the screen is the person the audience will see and hear. You must ask yourself: "Is this person convincing or boring?"

12.3 Practicing with an audience of one

Now you are ready for a version of almost prime time, a practice with another person sitting in judgment of your oratorical skills. Choose that person with care. You want constructive criticism, but you do not want the kind of person who enjoys pulling wings off a fly.

Although your self–confidence should now be much better after a series of solo practice sessions, augmented by audio and perhaps video reviews, your psyche may still be in a delicate position when it comes to hearing criticism. Neither do you want a person who simply cannot bring himself or herself to say an unkind word. Remember, you are steeling yourself for what could be a demanding presentation to a skeptical, questioning audience.

The reason you are practicing is to improve before the big day arrives. You want a person to tell you how you can improve, not one that says you are possibly one of the finest speakers in the world.

Candidates to play your audience of one. A spouse can be an excellent audience. Although he or she may not be well–versed in the subject matter of the upcoming presentation, a spouse is well–versed about you, and will be able to recognize if you are natural or stilted in your delivery. Additionally, a spouse has a vested economic interest in your success.

A colleague from work can be an excellent sounding board, but another word of caution. Depending on office politics and the competitive environment found in some companies, be careful whom you select. You do not want a person who could benefit by your presenting poorly.

A colleague who must also make presentations is a good candidate, for he or she realizes that helping you to improve will require you to reciprocate when that person must make a presentation.

Employ an audio recorder and, if possible, a video camera, in this session, just as you did in the solo practice. You will then have recorded the constructive comments made by your audience, in addition to seeing how you presented to another human being.

Go through the practice presentation from start to finish. If you keep stopping to make corrections, you'll run out of time, and your skill level will be uneven.

When you have finished this practice session and reviewed your audio– or videotape, you are now ready for your ultimate practice session – *The Murder Board.*

Chapter 13

The *Murder Board*: The Ultimate Rehearsal

A *Murder Board* is a rigorous practice, a simulation of the actual presentation to be made. It consists of colleagues role–playing the actual audience, asking the type of questions this audience is likely to ask.

As its rather macabre name implies, the *Murder Board* is intended to be more difficult and demanding than the actual presentation. In football terms, it is a full pads scrimmage.

If one is to become an effective and persuasive presenter, this realistic practice session is the most effective *shortcut* to speaking excellence. It allows you to make your mistakes when they don't count, increasing the odds that you will shine when the actual presentation is made.

13.1 The origin of the term *Murder Board*

The term *Murder Board* has its origins within the U.S. military, specifically within the extensive training system of the U.S. Army.

When a person has been selected to be an instructor at an Army school, he or she must go through a rigorous instructor training program.

Graduation and designation as an instructor is dependent not on passing a written test, but successful delivery of a 50 minute class from the curriculum of the school.

The audience for the would–be instructor are instructors who have already gone through their own *Murder Board*, and are determined that this would–be instructor will experience the same frustration and humiliation they did. They ask tough, but realistic, questions.

They confront the student instructor with the same pressures and distractions they have faced. At the end of the 50 minutes, the instructor gets a "thumbs up"–meaning he or she can now join this band of brothers and sisters on the platform, or a "thumbs down," meaning another opportunity to go through a *Murder Board.*

13.2 Lessons from the Pentagon

This realistic simulation has permeated military culture. As an example, when I ran the Defense Intelligence Agency's briefing team, we had three *Murder Boards* before the daily briefing to the Chairman of the Joint Chiefs of Staff.

The first one was at 5:30 AM, the second at 6:30 AM, and the third, in front of two General officers, one hour later. By the time my briefer or I was standing in front of the Chairman, those intense sessions had armed us with the right answers to virtually every conceivable question the Chairman was likely to ask.

This rigorous practice session, no less important in a business presentation with millions of contract dollars at stake, has two overriding objectives:

1. Honing delivery skills

2. Anticipating probable questions and objections so that succinct, accurate answers can be developed.

An effective *Murder Board* develops self–confidence in the presenter, and confidence of the senior executive that this presenter is well–prepared to tell the company's story.

13.3 Why have a *Murder Board?*

Many presenters, even while accepting the need to sharpen delivery skills, reject the idea of a *Murder Board*, confident they can anticipate the difficult questions likely to be asked, and therefore need not perform in front of others, especially their peers. These people may actually be displaying a false bravado to mask their discomfort at speaking in front of a group.

They are also very mistaken. I have given perhaps 2000 presentations, and always find it beneficial to conduct a *Murder Board* before an important presentation. The reason we need to test our presentation in front of others is that no matter how hard we try to think of tough questions that may be asked, a little censor in our mind generally provides only questions to which we already have answers. We need other minds to assist us.

I am in good company in believing in the need to have an intense practice session in front of others who are role–playing the audience to be faced. The man who possessed perhaps the greatest mind of the 20th

Century, Albert Einstein, realized that even he needed help. He once said:

> *"What a person does on his own, without being stimulated by the thoughts and experiences of others, is even in the best cases rather paltry and monotonous."*

The *Murder Board* is the presenter's equivalent of the actor's dress rehearsal, what lawyers do in preparing a witness to face cross–examination in a trial, what the flight simulator is to the pilot.

Just as with the actor, the witness, and the pilot, this simulation permits the presenter to learn from his/her mistakes, so that the actual presentation is more responsive to the informational needs of the audience and answers developed for likely questions to be asked.

The *Murder Board* enables you to visualize the presentation in advance. Not only is competence in speaking increased by such a rigorous practice, so too is self–confidence. Public speaking ranks high in the pantheon of phobias because of apprehension that one is going to be embarrassed by not being able to answer questions from the audience.

If, however, you have been able to anticipate questions, then you can develop answers ahead of time. If still another analogy is needed, think back to when you were in college or graduate school. Your GPA would probably have been higher if you could have seen the questions before the final exams. The *Murder Board* permits the presenter a legal and ethical look at he audience's "exam questions." The only obstacle to developing a question–anticipating *Murder Board* is your imagination and willingness to take hard hits in practice so you can be more effective in the actual presentation. In the next chapter, we'll show the seven steps for a successful *Murder Board*.

Chapter 14

Seven Steps to a Successful *Murder Board*

To have a successful and productive *Murder Board* enabling you to hone your skills and anticipate the difficult questions and comments requiring a response, I have found seven separate steps must be followed.

1. Recruiting
2. Sharing audience *Intelligence*
3. Role–playing by participants
4. Video–taping and/or audio–taping
5. Critique of presenter's *Style* and *Substance*
6. Recording on cards of all questions asked
7. Revision of the presentation

Let's take a look at each of these steps.

14.1 Recruiting

In recruiting people to be on your *Murder Board*, the best place to start is with knowledgeable colleagues. Request no more than four of these colleagues to be your simulated audience.

Keep in mind, however, that if these colleagues think that the objective of the *Murder Board* is only to help you look good, they probably will not want to give up their valuable time. You must give them an incentive tied to their self–interest.

They will have their own priorities. You should frame your request in such a way that these colleagues see a potential dividend accruing to them by investing their time. Remember from earlier in the book, and from your own experience, that *"What's in it for me?"* is the prime motivator for people to take action. You must find a way to have these colleagues believe they will gain by being in your simulated audience.

Reciprocity is the key. My advice is to recruit only people who themselves must make presentations. Then you say, "If you will be on my *Murder Board* now, I will be on yours when you must make a presentation." Presto. They see a potential benefit in the future by spending some time with you now.

Why only four people? One reason is to limit the debts you will have to pay in the future. You do not want to be spending all your available time being on the *Murder Boards* of others, and you certainly do not want to go back on your word.

Another reason is that most audiences you will face have no more than four key people. Having more than four colleagues helping you could result in a less–than–productive bull session, not a question–anticipating *Murder Board.*

14.2 Sharing *Audience Intelligence*

Because the purpose of a *Murder Board* is to create an environment for the presenter similar to the actual situation to be faced, it is important that those playing the members of the audience be armed with as much information about this audience as possible. That is where the intelligence collection discussed in Chapter 6 comes into play.

Participants must be steeped in the details of the issue being presented so they can put themselves in the mental framework of these participants. Information on the personal styles, idiosyncrasies, temperament, etc. of these audience members provides insight into how they will react to certain comments or proposals. Your colleagues can better role–play if they have this information. The more you know about personalities, the less surprised you will be in the presentation.

If the presentation is to be made internally, say to a Board of Directors or a Committee, participants in this practice session are likely to have valuable information to share with the presenter and other participants.

One of the reasons it is beneficial to recruit participants who present regularly is that they may have had the opportunity to present to the same people you are preparing to address. Colleagues can provide first–hand information on how your actual audience listens, questions, reacts, and interacts with fellow audience members.

14.3 Role–playing by participants

The success or failure of a *Murder Board* ultimately depends on its realism. The closer it is to the real thing, the better prepared will be the presenter. This realism, to a great degree, depends on the ability of your colleagues to get into the heads of the key players in your audience.

This does not mean having a great gift for acting or mimicry; but it does mean trying to think like the people in the audience so that statements made by the presenter will provoke questions likely to be asked by the actual audience.

After sharing all the intelligence gained on the audience, and eliciting from participants any insights they have on these people, assign specific roles to participants. If you are presenting to senior executives, you most certainly want a person to play the key decision maker.

If the CEO, for example, is an assertive person, try to have an assertive person play this role. If you know that the CEO tends to interrupt presentation with questions, request this role–player to do the same.

Remember that role–playing is very dependent on participants having, or having been provided, the most accurate and up–to–date intelligence on this audience.

If they do not have this information, the *Murder Board* could degenerate into a joking session which may relax you somewhat, but will not help you as much as a rigorous, no–holds barred simulation of that moment of truth when you stand in front of the real audience.

14.4 Video–taping / audio–taping

The actual conduct of the *Murder Board* is likely to not run smoothly, with various interruptions and discussions. Moreover, the presenter cannot be expected to remember all the comments, bits of advice, and questions asked. Consequently, much of the spontaneous, valuable information could be lost, even if someone is taking careful notes.

Consequently, it is beneficial to have both a video camera and a tape recorder running, during the practice presentation. This will provide a game film enabling you to see and hear yourself as your audience will see and hear you.

From the videotape you will learn if you are shifting from one side to the other, or grasping the lectern so your knuckles are white from pressure. Only when you see for yourself will you take corrective action.

Having an audio tape of your presentation allows you to focus on those vocal qualities such as monotone, inflection, pitch, speaking rate, "uh's" and "you knows," discussed in Chapter 18. Because the eye is so powerful, you may not notice any vocal problems when looking at the video tape. The audio tape will allow you to concentrate on your vocal qualities.

Perhaps the fundamental benefit of recording the practice session is that you will have a record of the questions asked in the give–and–take of the presentation, as well as your answers. Without an electronic record, the questions provoked by your presentation, and your answers, could be lost, thereby negating the benefits of the *Murder Board.*

14.5 Critique of presenter's *Style* and *Substance*

You have now completed your *Murder Board*, and, in the process, have used the valuable time of your colleagues. Now is the time to ask them for a robust critique of the substance of your presentation and your delivery style.

Keep the video camera and tape recorder rolling. These colleagues may be more expert in certain aspects of your presentation than you are, and you certainly want to tap into this expertise.

Additionally, they have just seen you presenting in a stressful environment – presenting before your colleagues may be more difficult than before a Board of Directors – and their comments on how you looked, how you sounded, and your overall presence can be invaluable.

Thank them for giving up their time, and remind them that you are ready to pay back when their time comes to make an important presentation.

You may wish to point out that you have indeed kept within the time limit promised, so that you establish a precedent for when your turn comes around to be a *Murder Board* participant.

14.6 Recording all questions asked on cards

Now it is just you, a VCR, a tape recorder and a stack of 3x5 cards. Why the cards? Because you are now going to go through the painful process of listening to how you answered the questions posed by your colleagues. Place each question asked on the front side of a 3x5 card. On the back – in pencil – place the answer you gave, or a better one if it occurs to you now, and it probably will. Why pencil? Because you are going to come up with better answers the more you think and research.

Reviewing the cards. When you are at home watching television, have that stack of cards nearby. When a commercial comes on the screen, select a card at random, look at the question, give an answer, and turn the card over. If your new answer is better than the one on the back of the card, make the correction.

Go through this procedure a few times, seeking each time to improve your answer so that you not only address the specifics of the question, but also find ways to reinforce your main points.

Following this procedure will do much to remove the fear of the unanticipated question, which has such a direct influence on fear of public speaking.

Keep the cards. Do not discard the cards after the presentation. They can serve as the foundation for your next presentation. If possible, catalog them by subject matter and place them in your database.

When you are called on at the last minute to make a short presentation, this card file can be a lifesaver and a career–enhancer, as you can quickly build a new presentation around one or two old questions.

People will think that you are indeed a silver–tongued orator who can put together a well thought out and extemporaneous presentation at the last minute. Let them think that. You will know that you are drawing on the "blood, sweat and tears" that went into your *Murder Board.*

14.7   Revise the presentation

Having completed your *Murder Board*, you are now faced with a dilemma. What do you do with all the new data generated by this most intense practice session? What if the audience doesn't ask the questions for which you have developed such great answers? Do you just leave this information in your files?

The answer is a resounding NO. Remember, your responsibility as a presenter is to provide maximum relevant information in minimum time in the clearest manner possible.

You must make a judgment as to which information best fits your objective and the informational needs of your audience. Some of the material you had originally had in your presentation may well have to be dropped, replaced by information that surfaced as a result of questions and discussions in the *Murder Board.*

An approach I have found useful is to time the *Murder Board* to be somewhat shorter than the time allocated for the actual presentation. This permits a time cushion that allows you to add new material without deleting too much of your original presentation.

It is best to schedule the *Murder Board* at least two days prior to the actual presentation so you have enough time to revise it to reflect the changes dictated by the questions and comments of your colleagues.

This will allow you to integrate the new information and answers that came about as a result of your practice session, and to develop new visuals, as well as giving you the opportunity to practice delivering the revised presentation.

14.8 The bottom line on the *Murder Board*

You need to conduct a *Murder Board* for the same reason that professional football teams, despite having injured players who could benefit from a rest, go through physically demanding practice sessions before the next game.

These athletes and their coaches realize the team will be better prepared by having practiced against what the coaches have anticipated, through scouting reports, the game plan of the opposing team. Presenters must follow the same logic.

It is foolish to deliver a "chips on the line" presentation without going through an intense *Murder Board*. The wise presenter realizes that he or she should put as much effort into the presentation as has been put into the product or service being sold.

In the next chapter which begins Part IV, we will look at how to convert your nervousness and stage fright into positive energy that translates into passion, intensity and enthusiasm.

Part IV

Presenting

Chapter 15

Converting Nervousness to Energy

At the risk of redundancy, I'll repeat what I pointed out in Chapter 1 – public speaking is the greatest fear in the United States. This was pointed out in the oft–quoted survey of 3,000 Americans, published by the Sunday Times of London on October 7, 1973. The finding of this survey has been verified by countless other surveys and studies.

The survey found that 41% of the respondents listed *"fear of public speaking"* as their number one apprehension, while 19% listed *"death."* This survey was later reported, and gained notoriety, in the *Book of Lists.*

In 1994, Dial Plus asked 1,000 Americans one of the most intrusive and inelegant questions in the history of survey research: "What makes you sweat the most?" (Remember, this was a soap company.)

To that question, 53% of the women, and 45% of the men, responded "speaking in public." When I learned of that survey I couldn't help but note how women were probably more honest than men on the issue, the male ego being less inclined to admit a weakness.

109

Despite the lack of scientific rigor in these and other surveys, I am inclined to believe them. In the hundreds of workshops I have conducted over the years, I have found a high percentage of very intelligent people becoming almost paralyzed at the prospect of making a speech. If you suffer from that same anxiety, rest assured you are in the main stream of the American public. This chapter will provide some advice on how to make this nervousness work to your advantage

15.1 Don't kill the butterflies

Among the physical manifestations of nervousness can be a queasiness frequently labeled "butterflies in the stomach." Someone in the field of speech training once said you didn't want to kill the butterflies, just get them to fly in formation.

Since that original and witty advice was first coined, it has had numerous self–described "authors." Most books and workshops on public speaking will offer it as the original insight of the expert who wrote that book or is conducting the workshop.

While I am certainly not claiming credit for that phrase, I certainly agree with its basic premise – that of controlling, not eliminating nervousness. I always find it disheartening to see or hear colleagues and competitors in the field of presentation skills training promise in their books or workshops that if you only buy their book or attend their workshop, you will never again fear speaking in public.

That is absolute rubbish. It is not only dishonest huckstering, it causes people to make overcoming stage fright their main objective. I have seen many nervous speakers do an outstanding job because they believed in their message, and I have seen speakers so calm it seemed rigor mortis had set in. Their calmness made them appear indifferent, and they bombed.

You want to be somewhat nervous. It releases the adrenaline that gets you "pumped," that shows passion and enthusiasm. It is the same as the pre–game jitters of athletes which allows them to perform.

They are converting nervousness to energy. Presenters must make the same conversion of what is frequently called stage fright into positive energy which demonstrates the presenter's belief in the message.

15.2 A trio of fears

There are essentially three reasons which result in presentation phobia. I address these in my workshops, showing how to control these fears so they work for, not against, the speaker. Below are those three fears, with recommended antidotes.

These remedies have worked for me, they have worked for my workshop participants, and they will work for you. You'll have those butterflies creating energy, not driving you crazy.

Fear of the unknown. As human beings, we tend to be more frightened of what we don't know. For presenters, the audience is the great unknown. You will wonder: "What do they expect of me? Do they know much more about the subject than I do, etc.?" You will have the tendency to magnify the knowledge of the audience at the expense of your own knowledge.

Antidote: Convert unknown to known. The more intelligence you gather on the audience (Chapter 6), and the more intensive your *Murder Board* (Chapters 13 and 14), the more the unknown will be converted to known.

You must guard against procrastination, however, because we tend to accomplish what is in our comfort zone, and put off more difficult tasks, such as a systematic *Audience Intelligence* collection and rigorous practice. Bite the bullet, and you will have those fears of the unknown dramatically reduced.

Fear of forgetting. When told they will have to make a presentation, most people are consumed by the fear their mind will go blank, and they will stand in front of the audience without the slightest idea of what they are to say.

The play it safe solution is to write out their presentation, and read it verbatim to the audience. This is normally a recipe for disaster. Audiences want to listen to a speaker who is connecting with them, is looking at them, not at sheets of paper. If you absolutely must read, follow the advice in Chapter 19.

Antidote: The two–card tango. The reality is that if you have practiced diligently, even a temporary "power outage" of your brain can be handled. The solution I have always used is what I call the *two–card tango*. Place a startling statistic or interesting fact that you have had to delete for reasons of time on a 3x5 card.

On the second card, place a bullet outline of the main points of your presentation. If convenient, place these cards in your pocket or on the lectern.

If the *My mind has gone blank syndrome* sets in, merely take both cards and say to the audience *"Let me digress for a moment and share with you..."* Then relate the information on the first card. If you have prepared well, your mind will probably kick back in, and you can continue where you left off. If it does not, slide the second card to the front, and look at the bullet points. Select one point and continue the presentation. Your audience will be none the wiser.

Although I always advocate honesty with your audience, I do not recommend that you say *"I forgot what I was going to say."* You may get temporary sympathy, but then audience members will wonder why they are sitting there if the issue is not important enough for the speaker to remember what he or she was saying.

Fear of unanticipated questions. Many people are not unduly worried about making a presentation, because they are "on their turf." These same people, however, are terrified at the prospect of answering questions. They believe they will be embarrassed by not being able to answer certain questions. These people are probably perfectionists, and believe they must be all−knowing on all things.

Antidote: Anticipate the questions. I realize that may sound simplistic, inviting the response "Yeah, right." Remember, however that learning what audience members will ask is precisely the goal of the *Murder Board* covered extensively in Chapters 13 and 14.

If you have acquired, as shown in Chapter 6, accurate intelligence on the audience's needs, concerns and problems, then you should be able to preempt certain questions, and anticipate others.

For perfectionists who think they must be able to answer every question, chill out. No one expects you to have all the information, but they do expect you to be honest. Don't give a false answer just to avoid the embarrassment of saying: *"I don't know."* That phrase, followed by *"but I'll get that information for you"* should be in every presenter's vocabulary. When you make that commitment, remember that you have a moral obligation to follow up and provide the answer, through some means, to the questioner, and perhaps to the entire audience.

113

The next chapter will show some rhetorical devices which can serve as a *shortcut* to persuasive eloquence in front of any audience.

Chapter 16

Shortcuts to Eloquence

You have probably had the experience of listening to a speaker who, even if you did not agree with that person's message, caused you to think, "this is an outstanding speaker." That speaker was probably using certain rhetorical devices that touched an internal chord.

Normally, such techniques are used by experienced speakers who have honed them over time. Yet you do not need to have delivered hundreds of presentations to develop the ability to incorporate rhetorical techniques which add grace, forcefulness and vividness to your presentation.

16.1 Eloquence

According to one of the most oft−quoted men of the 19th Century, Ralph Waldo Emerson, eloquence is

> *"the power to translate a truth into language perfectly intelligible to the person to whom you are speaking."*

Note that he said nothing about speaking in polysyllabic phrases aimed less at communicating than impressing. Truly eloquent speakers use short, direct, specific language aimed a their listeners. Winston Churchill's stirring speeches during World War II are prime examples of such language.

Eloquent speakers, like Churchill and John F. Kennedy, realize that the spoken word must appeal to the ear more than the eye, and nothing appeals more than repetition, rhythm and cadence. The eloquent presentation translates dull and colorless speech into words with punch which will be remembered.

In short, eloquence is where poetry and prose meet, where music and speech join. The means by which this is accomplished is by the adroit use of figures of speech, generally referred to as rhetorical devices.

16.2   Shortcuts to eloquence

The title of this chapter , and section, is my version of what are normally referred to as rhetorical devices. I do so for the simple reason that, adroitly employed, these techniques allow novices to appear as a very experienced speakers in the perception of the audience.

Inexperienced speakers can learn to incorporate into their presentations techniques that provide polish to what may be an otherwise pedantic effort. Below are five of these *shortcuts* that will let you implant your ideas into the collective mind of your audience.

16.3   Shortcut one: Repetition

Perhaps the most frequently used of these techniques is repetition of key words and key phrases to emphasize the presenter's message. An illustrative example is the famous 1963 speech by Dr. Martin Luther King, Jr. known as the *"I have a dream"* speech because he opened eight consecutive paragraphs with that phrase. Unless you believe you possess the oratorical skills of Dr. King, I would refrain from going that far in a business presentation. But a more limited repeating of key phrases does indeed add power to any presentation.

In a written essay, such repetition would be redundant. In a spoken presentation, it is an invaluable asset to hammer home the point you want your audience to grasp and act upon.

The King speech shows how repetition can allow a presentation to build to a crescendo. Repetition is frequently used at the beginning of a presentation to gain the audience' attention.

16.4   Shortcut two: The Rhythmic Triple

One again I am coining my own phrase. This technique, a variation of repetition, is generally called the *Rule of Three*, because it repeats, in threes, key words and phrases. I prefer the term *rhythmic triple* because this technique delivers a message with an ear–pleasing rhythm and cadence in the beat of three.

The speaker using this technique drives home his or her point with three words, three sentences, three phrases. "Threes" tend to reinforce, because, for reasons no one fully understands, people remember best when they hear repetition in a series of three. Repeating twice is too little, four or more two much (unless you are a Dr. Martin Luther King, Jr.).

Churchill was a great user of the rhythmic triple, as when he said of the Royal Air Force,

117

"Never in the field of human conflict has <u>so much</u> been owed by <u>so many</u> to <u>so few</u>

He could have said *"We owe a great debt to the fliers of the RAF in the saving of Britain."* Would this phrase have been as memorable?

In July 2002, Governor Mark Schwieker of Pennsylvania used the rhythmic triple in demanding an explanation about safety procedures from the company that owned the mine where nine miners were entombed before being miraculously rescued. The Governor said, with considerable emotion, that the company owed an explanation *"To the miners, to their families and to me."*

Where to find examples of the Rhythmic Triple. You local library will have copies of *Vital Speeches,* published every two weeks. Peruse speeches made by prominent business and government leaders, and you'll find numerous examples of the rhythmic triple. You can then adapt these to your own requirements.

You can also use a thesaurus or synonym finder to aid you in finding related words to link together in developing your rhythmic triple.

A word of caution. This is a such a powerful device that employing it almost guarantees your point will be remembered by your audience. So be careful when employing. You may wish to take a lesson from the experience of the first President George Bush.

At the 1988 Republican Convention, then Vice–president Bush, against the advice of some of his economic advisers, used a double "Rhythmic Triple" in saying *"Read My Lips: No New Taxes."* Had he wanted to be vague, while still voicing his opposition to new taxes, he could have said *"At this point in time, I assure you that I have no intention of engaging in any new revenue enhancement devices."*

Those in the Convention audience, and Republicans watching on television, would have known he was promising to not raise taxes. The cumbersome phrase, however, would not have been memorable.

He was elected President that year, of course, but proceeded to raise taxes in 1990. During his bid for reelection in 1992, the Democratic Party kindly reminded the electorate of his double *rhythmic triple* . Had Mr. Bush not been so eloquent in 1988, he might have been reelected in 1992.

As with all these devices, don't overdo it. You do not want to be so engrossed in "sounding" eloquent that you do not get your message across. Too many *triples* is similar to putting too much seasoning on food. It will take a lot of experimenting, but once you are comfortable with this technique, you have added a powerful weapon to your speaking arsenal.

16.5 Shortcut three: Rhetorical Question

This technique, where you pose a question and then provide the answer, can be used to draw an audience that may have "wandered off" back to the speaker's message. It can also be used to force the audience to reflect actively on what you have said, not just passively listen.

You can also use it to lead into a summary of key points, as well as a transition from one key point to another.

If you are making a presentation to a small group, and notice that a person is sleeping, you may wish to move close to that person, pose a question, wait about two seconds, and then provide the answer.

The result will be an audience member who is now wide awake and very grateful that it was a rhetorical question, not one demanding an answer. Be cautious, however, in using this technique when presenting to a senior executive who might have dozed off. It will be more prudent to let others wake him or her up.

In drafting the presentation, look for places to insert rhetorical questions, then merely convert declarative sentences into question form, and you have automatically changed the cadence of your presentation. You also keep the audience attentive, because they will not know if it is a rhetorical question or one where you expect someone to respond.

16.6 Shortcut four: The Pause

Inserted strategically and occasionally dramatically, a *pause* is an effective means to call attention to a point just made, allowing the information to be absorbed before the next point is articulated. Developing the technique of the *pause* also forces a speaker with a tendency to speak quickly to slow down. The pause can be effectively used to substitute for "uh" when you are reaching for just the right word.

Think of your presentation as vintage wine being poured into the small wine glasses of your audience's retention. You cannot pour constantly, or much of the wine will spill on the table. Stop pouring for about two seconds to permit another glass to be placed under the bottle.

16.7 Shortcut five: Chiasmus

Chiasmus, a term from ancient Greece, is the reversal of phrases within the sentence in the form of AB–BA. A very familiar use of this technique was in President John F. Kennedy 1961 inaugural address, when he said,

"Ask not what your country can do for you. Ask what you can do for your country."

Had he phrased this call to arms as a simple declarative sentence such as *"You should ask how you as citizens you can help your county in its time of need,"* it would have been far less effective.

If you would like to receive a weekly history lesson and example of Chiasmus and other figures of speech, send an E-mail to Dr. Mardy Grothe at chiasmus-on@mail-list.com requesting a free subscription to his educational E-mail service. Every Sunday this indefatigable researcher will send you examples from history of the use of chiastic and other devices which will give you ideas how to enliven your own presentations.

There are a number of other rhetorical devices, but the ones provided in this chapter provide a solid start. Learn to integrate them into your presentations and meetings, and you will be thought of as a very experienced and eloquent speaker, even if you are not yet at this stage.

In the next chapter, we'll look at how to use, and not misuse, visual aids, including the ubiquitous *PowerPoint*.

Chapter 17

Visual Aids to Support, not Distract

PowerPoint is the most powerful graphics tool available to presenters. It is relatively easy to use, and has become a metaphor for graphics programs, much as Xerox has become the generic word for photocopying documents.

17.1 An overview of visual aids

Before discussing how *PowerPoint* can help or, unfortunately, harm a presentation, let's discuss visuals in general.

People learn best when they can see as well as hear. Visual aids, however, must support the presentation, not be the presentation. Many presenters use visuals as a crutch, not an aid. Because visuals appeal to the eye, they draw attention away from the speaker, and the presenter wishing to establish strong credibility should not be relegated to the role of Master of Ceremonies for a projector.

You must, of course, always keep the audience in mind. Can a myopic person sitting at the most distant point from the screen easily read the words? When in doubt, always use larger fonts. No presenter is ever criticized because the lettering is too large.

Don't put the visual cart before the content horse. When preparing a presentation, develop the content before you design the visuals. Your objective in using any visual aids must be to design and utilize them so they reinforce, not detract from, your presentation.

Many presenters, taking the lazy way, find old visuals and build the presentation from them. Although this may be necessary when you have been given virtually no time to prepare, it stilts the creative process and can result in a stale presentation.

You can certainly look at old visuals (and I am a believer in not deleting or throwing away visuals) to give you some ideas. Just don't bend the new content to fit the old visual.

Presenter, screen and pointer. Stand to the left of the screen (from the audience's perspective) because you are the principal visual, and audiences read from left to right. They will look at you first, then the visual on the screen. If you are on the right of the screen, they will be distracted by looking at you, then back to the screen, then back to you.

To avoid reading every word on the screen, position yourself so you are not blocking the screen, then keep your feet pointed towards the audience. You can then turn slightly towards the screen with your upper body, but if you do not make the pivot with your feet, this position will be so uncomfortable that you will return to having eye contact with the audience, not the screen.

123

When standing to the left of the screen, and far enough away to avoid blocking the view of any audience members, you may need to use a pointer. My advice is to not use a laser pointer. Even the calmest presenter will have some shakiness, and this hand movement will be exaggerated by the little red dot jumping about the screen

I also advise not to use the expandable pointer, which has become so popular. Despite its inherent "coolness," you will probably expand and contract it continually, as if you are playing an accordion. Several such moves will be very distracting to audience members who may begin counting them, or wonder what song you are playing.

My advice? Stick with a wooden, 36 inch pointer, even at the risk of appearing old–fashioned.

Using an assistant. If a colleague is assisting you by running the projector, the two of you must practice coordinating words and slides. A technique that can facilitate blending the oral message with visual is for the presenter occasionally to ask a rhetorical question, with the slide then appearing on the screen providing the answer. Do this especially for the most important points for the audience to comprehend.

17.2   Overhead transparencies

An "oldie but goodie" means of transferring information visually to the audience is the overhead transparency. This system is reliable, relatively inexpensive, and can be shown with only a minimum dimming of lights.

The principal disadvantage is that last–minute changes are not as easy to accomplish as they are with *PowerPoint*, and the audience may think you are not keeping up with technology, thereby impacting on your credibility.

When using bullet outlines or laundry lists on overhead transparencies, a frequent problem is that audience members may concentrate on, say, the fourth line while the speaker is referring to the first line.

To focus the audience's attention where you want it, use the revelation technique. Cover all the lines you are not addressing with a piece of paper, and reveal each line as you come to it in the presentation. This, of course, can be done automatically with animation in *PowerPoint*.

Keep the lighting as bright as possible, but don't wash out the screen. A darkened room, required when using 35mm slides, is an invitation to sleep for even the most attentive audience members. If there is a bank of lights in front of the screen, see if can be disabled.

Projectors. Unless the projector is very new, the image on the screen may be crooked, even when the transparency is placed properly and squared away on the projector. To compensate for the bias, tape strips on the projector and place your transparencies on this new template.

A disadvantage of most overhead projectors is that they can block the view of some audience members. Keep this in mind as you are setting up and arranging the seating.

The overlay technique. In depicting complex data with a number of variables, use large lettering to facilitate audience comprehension, and consider using the overlay technique.

This technique is especially valuable for quantitative presentations explaining data through several variables. The same procedure, of course, can be used with vertical or horizontal bar or line graphs. The same procedure, of course, can be used with vertical or horizontal bar or line graphs.

Place the basic drawing on one transparency and put additional data on other sheets. These can be superimposed on the basic transparency. Audience members can more readily grasp relations among data points when they are shown sequentially. They can become confused if all the data is presented to them simultaneously.

Talk first, show later. Most people use transparencies as their notes, placing the slide on the projector and then referring to the data points or words on the transparency. An effective alternative I find useful is the *talk first, show later* method.

Explain the points you wish the audience to retain so members can develop an image in their mind, then show the transparency. The information is thereby reinforced because you have caused the audience to think, not merely receiving the information passively.

This reverse from the normal procedure also benefits by being different from the way audiences are accustomed to having overhead transparencies shown to them.

17.3   The promise and perils of *PowerPoint*

Two principles to keep in mind when using *PowerPoint*;

> **DO NOT** use all the "bells and whistles."
> **DO** use some of the "bells and whistles."

I have seen *PowerPoint* presentations which were a testimony to the ingenuity of the software developers at Microsoft – arrows doing a double back flip as they flew onto the screen, words appearing to fly off the screen toward the audience, vibrant colors I had never seen before, and so on.

The problem with these presentations is that I could not concentrate on the substantive content the presenter was attempting to convey, so impressed was I with the "pizzazz" of the slides bursting into my consciousness. I still remember all the bells and whistles; I have no recollection of the points the presenter was making.

I have also attended presentations in which bullet outlines came onto the screen all at once, as they would with an overhead transparency not using the revelation technique. As I watched these bullets assault me all at once, I was distracted by the thought that $5,000.00 worth of computer and projector were being used to convey information the way it could be provided the audience with a $200.00 overhead projector.

It is best to bring bullets on the screen as they are being addressed by the presenter. *PowerPoint* allows you to do this seamlessly, even dimming the previous bullet to allow it to stay on the screen.

17.4 Maximizing *PowerPoint*

Fonts. A problem presented by any computer program is the multiplicity of fonts available. Occasional use of different fonts can enliven a page or screen, but using several types can make the speaker appear to be a graduate of the ransom note school of presentations. Use font size large enough to be seen in the back of the room. This forces you to not put too much information on one slide.

AutoContent Wizard/templates. For a person who is new to *PowerPoint*, the AutoContent Wizard and template capabilities can make the rookie appear the veteran. Don't let your ego get in the way – your job is to develop interesting and compelling content. You are an expert on your field; take advantage of the experts who have developed the built–in formats.

Transitions. Be careful with the transitions from one slide to the next. *PowerPoint* will help you gain audience attention, but, as pointed out above, overly flashy transitions and animations can also annoy and distract the audience.

Colors. Use colors that do not clash. I prefer the deep blue background, gold headlines, and white text. These colors match well and are not distracting. Avoid mixing extreme colors such as fuchsia and orange. Keep in mind that approximately 8% of the American population has a degree of color blindness with regard to red and green.

17.5   The bottom line on *PowerPoint*

Let this outstanding program work for you but always keep in mind that, for serious audience members, content trumps pizzazz. As you are developing your presentation, always remember that your job is to transfer information from you to your audience. *PowerPoint* can help you implant this information so your audience will remember it, but excessive reliance on the flash aspects of the program could result in your audience recalling how great were your visuals, but being oblivious to your message.

Above all, remember that you are the messenger, and *PowerPoint* exists only to help you. In the next chapter, we'll discuss the most important visual in any presentation – you!

Chapter 18

How You Look and Sound

A presentation is more than the sum of the words spoken. The perception by audience members of how the speaker looks and sounds has a decided impact, both positive and negative, on how the message is accepted. A trite but true adage is *"You cannot not communicate."*

In this chapter I want to show the relation between appearance, voice and body language, and how they influence audiences. Despite what we would like to think – that it is the lucidity of our logic that persuades an audience to our point of view – empirical research on group behavior suggests strongly that non–verbal communication has a significant impact on how audiences interpret our presentation.

When you have an important message, don't shoot yourself in the foot by delivering it with flawed non–verbal communication. A message vital to the audience but delivered in a boring monotone, perhaps being read from a text or words on a screen, can easily turn off an audience. There is little doubt that a degree of acting and stagecraft are a part of even the most serious presentation.

Here are some tips to assist you in being *non–verbally fluent.*

18.1 Appearance and dress

The "first impression" factor. The audience will make an immediate judgment about you by your clothing and grooming. You do not want the audience's memory of how you dressed to overshadow the intellectual content of your presentation.

Dress. If you are presenting to a business group, members of this audience are not expecting you to make a fashion statement–they are expecting you to dress in a conservative manner consistent with the message you are delivering and the nature of this audience. A useful rule of thumb is dress one step up from the audience. If they are in sport coats, wear a suit. If they are in very casual attire, wear a sport coat, or for women, perhaps a blazer.

Advice for women. Women have much more flexibility than do men, and can dress conservatively but stylishly. My advice is to not wear excessive jewelry that may be distracting. Earrings that are very large and/or reflect the light can distract. If you are speaking from a raised platform, skirt length can also be distracting. Conservative, but not dowdy, is best.

Women tend to wear shoes that are stylish, even if they are not comfortable. Ill–fitting shoes, however, can prove very disconcerting to the woman presenter who is on her feet for a lengthy presentation and question–and–answer session.

Advice for men. Men generally do not have as good a sense of style and color coordination as do women. Generally speaking, dark suits are better than light (although in the Summer light–colored suits are acceptable). Neatly–pressed white shirts are advisable, although the blue shirt with white collar favored by many television anchors is stylish. Ties should be conservative, as you never wish to have audience members distracted by overly "flashy" neckwear. The traditional red "power tie" is always a good bet.

Keep your suit coat buttoned, and your tie centered. The buttoned coat shows respect for your audience. The open coat is can be interpreted by some audience members as connoting a casual approach to an issue they take seriously. A tie that is oft–center can be very distracting, not just for "neat freaks" in the audience.

Shoes should match the suit (no brown shoes with dark suit), they should not be run down at the heels, and should be shined.

18.2   Body language

Studies indicate that when people detect a difference between the non–verbal body language and the spoken language, they tend to believe the non–verbal. A speaker saying *"I'm very happy to be with you,"* while wringing his or her hands, may not be considered a happy camper by the audience. Hand wringing may also be perceived by the audience as nervousness generated by delivering message that is not true, *even if it is.*

Avoiding "happy feet." A stressful situation such as speaking before a group activates adrenaline. This can manifest itself in pacing back and forth. While it is best to have movement, rather than appear like a statue, make this movement with a purpose. If not tied to a lectern, move toward the audience, and then back up, never turning your back on the group. Be aware, of course, of any furniture that could painfully interrupt your backward movement.

Gestures. Movement of the hands and arms should be natural and energetic, but not so expansive as to make you appear to be a televangelist who has had too much coffee.

131

The hands and arms can serve as visual exclamation points for your words. Just don't overdo them, because you are not playing Hamlet when making a presentation. Imagine you are speaking to a friend on your cell phone.

Gestures can reduce a monotone. It is almost impossible to speak in boring tones when gesturing, and it is very difficult to avoid a monotone when your arms are at your side.

Eye contact. Americans are distrustful of a person who does not *look them in the eyes*. Good eye contact helps a speaker *reach out* to an audience and establish the human contact which is so much a part of the oral presentation.

Pick a person (preferably friendly) in each section of he room and rotate your gaze around the room by having a brief conversation (no more than two sentences) with that person.

This will help you to connect with the audience, and it will calm your nerves. However, when giving a presentation to, say, the CEO of a company, devote most of the *eye contact time* to this person, breaking contact periodically to look at other people giving that senior person a rest from intensive eye contact with you, the presenter.

Facial expression. Audience members will be looking at your face when you speak. They will instinctively note any discrepancy between the message you are conveying and the expression on your face. Again, the speaker saying how happy he or she is to be speaking, but who accompanies this message with a poker face and a monotone, is inviting skepticism.

If you are providing bad news, but doing so with a smile, audience members will detect a mixed message. Congruency between message, body language and facial expression goes a long way toward establishing credibility.

18.3 The voice

The voice does the heavy lifting in any presentation. Some people are blessed with mellifluous voices which are so pleasing to the ear that audiences may not even pay attention to the thoughts being expressed.

Many of us must actively guard against the problems of accents, problems associated with tone and pitch, a too fast or too slow rate of delivery, speaking too loudly or (more commonly) too softly. Then, of course, there is the bane of all speakers, the use of those abominable fillers, *"uh"* and *"y'know."*

Below are some of the most common vocal problems along with advice on how to correct them.

Regional accent. Accents in the United States frequently cause more concern among self-conscious presenters than it does with audiences listening to them. Many presenters feel an undeserved sense of inferiority if their accent is distinctly different from the accents of those to whom they are speaking.

You should be careful about your diction and pronunciation, but realize that television has brought all accents into our homes, and audiences are accepting of these differences. Still, the closer you can come to mainstream English – perhaps like that of a television news-reader – the better off you will be.

Foreign accent. Americans, as a rule, do not have a good ear for foreign accents, and this can cause problems for the non-native speaker of English. If he or she has a strong accent, their American audiences may not understand essential parts of the presentation. If audience members cannot understand what the presenter is saying, the message will not be conveyed. An accent reduction coach should be consulted.

Tone. Men have a tendency to speak in a monotone, which can be very annoying and boring. If you have this problem, as was noted in Chapter 12, practice speaking with a tape recorder, placing emphasis on verbs and other words which connote action and movement.

Underlining or printing these words in bold type can assist in overcoming this mannerism. Women generally do not have the monotone problem, as they generally speak with inflection. Their problem is more likely to be pitch.

Pitch. Too high a pitch can be irritating to the human ear. Women presenters may wish to lower their pitch using as role–models the late Congresswoman Barbara Jordan, former U.N. Ambassador Jeane Kirkpatrick, and poet Maya Angelou, all of whose voices are feminine, but within the comfort range of the human ear.

Rate of delivery. A good rate of delivery is approximately 150 words per minute, but even this should be varied. The delivery rate should also be adapted to the audience. A group in New York would be irritated by slow delivery, while an audience in Dallas would be put off by a machine–gun delivery.

Volume. Although some men speak at too low a volume, it is more a problem for women. To develop higher volume, ask a colleague to stand in the back of a large room, such as an auditorium, holding his or her arm at waist level. As you speak, the colleague then raises his or her arm until you reach the level at which the colleague can comfortably hear you. Maintain that volume, and you will now know at what level you should speak.

134

"Uh's" **and** *"y'knows."* These sounds, which in a perfect world would be expunged from our oral vocabulary, can destroy an otherwise well–crafted presentation. There are variants to these utterances, but concentrating on eliminating them would be a good start to becoming a better speaker.

Audience members are sensitive to these sounds, and may start counting how many times the presenter uses them. When attention is focused on counting, little attention can be devoted to absorbing the substance of the presentation

A drill to help you reduce *"uh's"* and *"y'knows"* in your delivery is to have colleagues in a practice session shout *"Uh!"* when you utter that sound, and *"No, we don't!"* when you say *"Y'know."*

I use this exercise in my workshops, and it works wonders. People must be aware that hey are using these sounds before they can take steps to reduce their use.

Advice from Maya Angelou. The poet Maya Angelou, singled out above as a role–model for women presenters, is gifted with one of the most pleasant voices to be heard today. She realizes this, and quite properly takes advantage of this God–given gift. She has written that

> *"Words mean more than what is set down on paper.*
> *It takes the human voice to infuse them with deeper*
> *meaning."*

Amen.

In the next chapter, we'll turn to the challenge posed when you are required to read verbatim the presentation.

Chapter 19

When You *Must* Read

Let me start with a bias I believe is shared by many. I have an intense dislike of listening to a speech or presentation that is read. My immediate reactions are

1. To wonder who actually wrote the speech,
2. Prefer being given a copy to read at my leisure,
3. Be bored and inattentive as the speaker drones on.

Having gotten that off my chest, I'll now say that there are times when a speaker has no alternative – he or she must read the speech. That is the sour lemon we must all accept from time to time. In this chapter I'll show you how to make lemonade. (Not very original, I admit, but it does fit.)

I recommend that you read Chapter 10 again, which described the steps to draft for the ear and not the eye, essential when you must read to an audience.

19.1   When reading is necessary

When the President of the United States speaks from the Oval Office, or delivers the State of the Union address, his words have been crafted and vetted carefully. A casual ad lib or personal aside could have international ramifications.

On these occasions, of course, the President is reading from a TelePrompTer, but the television audience has the feeling he is speaking extemporaneously to them. There are some other instances when reading is required.

1. When the Chairman of the Federal Reserve speaks on the economy, these words are likewise carefully chosen and delivered verbatim – lest there be a global stock market crash.

2. A news–reader on television or radio is under severe time limits, and must read from a TelePrompTer or script.

3. Time constraints for business presentations are a factor that could ultimately cause a presentation to be read, as could a situation where the scheduled presenter is indisposed, and a last minute substitute must step in.

4. When you are told by your boss that these are the "golden words" and no deviation is permitted.

19.2   Why many presenters choose to read

Many presenters, unfortunately, choose to read their presentation, even when it is not required. For the most part, they do so because of their fear of speaking. They are afraid they will forget what they were going to say. Having a written text in front of them is a security blanket.

Anecdotes abound about corporate CEOs and politicians who read their speechwriter–prepared presentations, only to stumble through words with which they were not familiar or in some other way provide comic relief to their audiences. Their problem, of course, was that they were not trying to be funny.

They walked to the lectern, kept their eyes on the text, and never saw the audience until finished. The following true story is frequently told in Washington: A Senator (who shall remain anonymous) was handed his speech by a staff member just before mounting the podium.

Unfortunately for the Senator, he failed to note that the first page was the press release touting how his remarks were greeted with thunderous applause. The hapless Senator read the press release, to the dismay of his staff as his audience roared with laughter.

I'm going to provide two solutions you can use when you are either tempted or directed to read verbatim from a script. You'll find that these alternatives will enable you to have a "crutch" without boring your audience.

For those who are directed to follow a corporate line, either of these solutions will get you off the hook. I've used both solutions, and they work.

19.3 Solution one: Doctor the script

If you are preparing to deliver a written report orally you are not necessarily in a no–win situation. You can re–write it to put the written information into spoken language. Changing how the words appear on your script can help you sound more natural, sincere, and spontaneous.

If you cannot alter the words, alter the formatting. A written report is quite naturally written for the eye – the way we are accustomed to writing, single space and in 12 point font. If, however, you change the formatting, a more natural delivery will ensue. Your eye contact with the audience will improve, and you will sound more conversational, yet you are still delivering the words the audience must hear.

You'll find that this requires a good bit of pre–presentation work on your part, but the payoff is that you'll look more in command, and less of a robot reading words written by another person.

Here are some ways to doctor any script; I found them useful when I had to read words that had been "blessed" by a higher authority. They are purely mechanical, and do not alter those words which have been mandated by your superiors.

Double space, 24 point font. You will not be able to read as easily when making the presentation as you can while sitting at your desk. A memo or speech written in conventional 12 point font will cause numerous blunders when you have to read it from the lectern. The stress of speaking will affect your reading ability, and the lighting at the lectern may make reading difficult.

My advice is to use 24 point font, bold type, and double space. You may think that is too large a font. When you stand at a lectern with a dim light that may even reflect on the paper, you'll be glad you have large print to read.

Use upper and lower case type. Some believe typing in all capital letters will make it easier to read. Not so. We are accustomed to reading primarily in lower case.

Wide margins, short paragraphs, bottom third blank. Complement the 24 point font with wide margins so that your eyes need not travel from left to right on the page. When possible, create paragraphs of no more than six lines.

Coupled with the six words across resulting from the large font, you will be able to take in the words with out moving your eyes from left to right. The paragraph breaks will enable you to have more eye contact with the audience. Large margins will provide space for notes on both sides of the text that cue you when to pause, when to look at the audience, and so on.

Leave the bottom third of the page blank, so you will not be required to lower your head too much. That will also facilitate having more eye contact with audience members.

Underline, highlight or bold type for emphasis. When you speak extemporaneously or conversationally, you will be more inclined to use natural inflection. When reading, you are likely to read aloud the way you read silently – in a monotone.

To avoid doing this, underline key words and phrases requiring emphasis with a highlighter or use bold type.

Practice with tape–recorder/video–camera. In Chapters 12, 13 and 14 I urged you to use a tape–recorder when drafting and practicing. I advise the same when preparing for a presentation that must be read. Read through the entire presentation, and then listen to yourself.

140

You want to sound enthused and passionate about your subject. Above all, you want to avoid the droning on in a monotone that is the fundamental complaint of audiences forced to endure a presentation that is read from a script.

19.4   Solution two:
Hand out the presentation, then go to Q&A

A far less complicated alternative is to have the presentation prepared for the eye (12 point font, one inch margins) as a monograph which you then provide to all audience members. Deliver a brief extemporaneous *oral executive summary*, then turn the session into a question–and–answer session.

By doing this, you have the best of both worlds. You comply with the requirement to provide the audience with the blessed words, but you avoid boring them to death.

Whether you choose solution one or solution two you will be far better off than if you read in what will probably inevitably degenerate into a boring monotone. And so will your audience.

In the next chapter, we'll tackle that occasion which causes so much apprehension among presenters–the Q & A session.

Chapter 20

Question Time: Your Golden Opportunity

Why is it that many people dread the *Question–and–Answer session*, when it is so close to the conversational mode with which we are so accustomed? Probably because they believe they are no longer in control of the agenda, and they run the risk of appearing less knowledgeable on the subject than they were in making the actual presentation.

The *Q&A session* should, however, be thought of by the well–prepared speaker as an excellent and interactive opportunity to drive home points the speaker wants to emphasize to the audience. It is where you show to audience members that you can communicate as well on their turf as you can in your prepared presentation.

20.1 Fear of the unanticipated question

From my experience in training executives, diplomats, engineers and lawyers, this particular fear has its root in the fear of being asked a question and not having the foggiest idea how to answer. Many presenters believe they must be able to answer all questions, or they have failed. Absolutely not!

The simple solution when you don't know the answer is to say *"I don't know, but I'll get that information for you."* Write the question down, to demonstrate your sincerity. Make sure you do get the information to the questioner, and, if feasible, to the entire group.

The best way to counter the fear of unanticipated questions, of course, is to make them anticipated by means of a thorough *Murder Board*. Engaging in this realistic simulation (Chapters 13 and 14) will enable the speaker to anticipate many of the most likely questions his or her presentation will provoke. It will also cause the speaker's confidence to soar, somewhat like knowing the exam questions in college before an important test.

20.2 Driving home the *Bottom Line*

A great benefit of the Q&A session is that audience questions can provide the opportunity deliver a mini–presentation that focuses the audiences' attention on those points the speaker wants understood and acted upon.

Listen carefully for the nuance of the question, for some in an audience are inarticulate in asking their question. If necessary, rephrase the question, and ask the questioner if that is a fair summation of the question. As you are listening, and repeating, be scanning your internal data base to see what of your main points you can insert in the answer to reinforce your message.

As a general rule, keep answers short so as to not enter into a dialogue with the questioner to the exclusion of the rest of the audience. By repeating the question, you permit all in the audience to hear it, in addition to giving you the opportunity to be thinking and refining your answer. A thoughtful pause before answering the question adds to your credibility.

20.3 Non–verbal communication

Maintain eye contact with the questioner when he/she is speaking, and at the outset of your answer. After about two sentences, look at other members of the audience. As you are ending your answer, look at the questioner.

While the question is being asked, you should assume a relaxed position, with your elbows bent and your hands clasped lightly at waist level. Avoid folding your arms across your chest, as that could suggest defensiveness to people who have read too many books on body language.

Be careful about nodding as you listen to the question. This is a habit we develop in conversations, and it shows we are listening and tracking the question. If the questioner, however, suddenly takes on a critical tone at variance with the message you have delivered, continued affirmative nodding on your part could cause audience members to think you are now contradicting yourself.

20.4 Priming the pump

When you say something like *"I'd be delighted to answer any questions my presentation may have provoked,"* and no hands are raised, you may feel you have really bombed out. Not necessarily so.

Many people are reluctant to ask the first question after hearing a presentation because asking a question is, after all, *speaking in public.*

All the fears associated with this affects audience members as well as presenters. Moreover, people realize they did not pay attention to every word spoken, and are concerned their daydreaming will be revealed if they ask a question about an issue covered in detail in the presentation.

The standard way to get around this problem, one that I used in those infrequent times when I was greeted by silence, is to say, *"A question I frequently receive is...".* Then I posed a question, provided a succinct answer, and then said: *"Who has the next question?"*

This technique works most of the time. If, however, there are no questions, just say something along the line of *"Well, I'm glad we are all on the same page, and I thank you very much for giving me the time to discuss this issue."*

20.5 Dealing with belligerent or filibustering questioners

When confronted with a belligerent questioner, remain calm, and certainly do not become embroiled in an argument. But at the same time, you do not wish to be so conciliatory that you appear to have no convictions.

You must stand your ground, using reason. If a questioner persists, a useful technique is to invite the person to discuss the issue with you after the presentation *"because I am very interested in your point of view."*

A questioner who asks a long–winded question my be hostile, or merely wants to show off his/her knowledge to you and the rest of the audience. If you sense the audience is becoming irritated with the mini–presentation being given by a questioner, you must politely interrupt.

You could smile and ask, *"Is there a question hidden in there somewhere?"*

If the questioner does not take the hint, interrupt more firmly, saying that there are many people in the audience who have questions, and you wish to give them the opportunity to have their say.

20.6 Beware the hidden premise

A variant of the belligerent questioner is the person who attempts to trap you by seeming to agree with your basic argument, but in reality wants to trip you up. They may lead into the question with a phrase such as *"Given the fact that...,"* followed by a negative interpretation of your position.

When you see that the question has a hidden premise, challenge the questioner immediately, saying, *"No, that is not what I said. Let me clarify and reemphasize my basic point."*

20.7 Avoiding a dialogue

Because of the habits we develop in conversations of maintaining eye contact with the person to whom we are speaking, we run the risk of engaging in a dialogue with the questioner, to the exclusion of other members of the audience.

You want to include everyone in your answer. Do this with your eyes. As you start answering the questioner, look at him or her for perhaps one or two sentences. Then look at another person, and then another. Come back to the questioner when you are completing your answer, and by tone of voice, indicate that is the full answer.

Then break eye contact, and look for another question. If you continue looking at the questioner, he or she may feel compelled to ask another question. You want to spread the questions around the room.

20.8   Ending the Q&A session

Most people end their presentations when they have been thanked by the moderator or senior person. This is wasting a valuable opportunity to reinforce the main points you have conveyed. The next chapter will show how to fire a *Final Arrow* that drives home this main point.

Chapter 21

Firing the *Final Arrow*

Perhaps the most counter–intuitive aspect of my system is the concept of the *Final Arrow*. Employing this technique, when appropriate, can be among the most important elements of your presentation. Note that I said *when appropriate*. You must know when to fire, and when it is more prudent to keep that last arrow in your quiver.

Just what do I mean by the *Final Arrow*? Recall that in Chapter 7, I discussed the courtroom principle of *Primacy* and *Recency*, based on the empirical evidence that people tend to remember what they hear first, and what they hear last, leading to the importance placed by trial lawyers on their *opening statement* and *closing argument.*

That, of course, is the same reason I place so much emphasis on the *3–1–2 System* of structuring the presentation so that the concluding words audience members hear (3) will contain the message that moves them to take the action desired by the speaker.

During the question and answer session, the discussion may have ranged far and wide from the focus of the presentation. That is where the *Final Arrow* comes into play, and why it can, under certain circumstances, have a profound impact on the success or failure of a presentation.

21.1 The quiver

Think of having a quiver of informational arrows on your back as you prepare to deliver your presentation. You fire your first volley to gain the attention of the audience in your *Return On Investment* opening, flowing from the (1) of your structure. You show the audience you know their problem and you will be furnishing a solution.

Then you fire those arrows containing your supporting data, the (2) information which is the "meat" of your presentation. Finally, you launch the (3) arrow, driving home your point and probably setting the stage for questions from the audience. This is where focus can be lost.

After you have answered questions from the audience, you *may* have an opportunity to fire the last arrow in your quiver, a distillation of the main point of your presentation, the point that causes the audience to take the action you have advocated.

21.2 Key elements of the *Final Arrow*

No new information. Because this element of the presentation will come after the formal close – someone will have thanked you – it is imperative that you <u>not</u> introduce new information. This is the opportunity to reiterate and reinforce the main points of your presentation.

Deliver while doing *housekeeping* duties and in *fifteen seconds*. Audiences, particularly in business and government, are not accustomed to hearing a speaker continue after being thanked for his or her

149

presentation. They do realize, however, that notes must be gathered, laptops closed, etc. Fire your *Final Arrow* while accomplishing these tasks and maintaining eye contact with the key decision–maker. By doing this in fifteen seconds or less, you come in under the radar, getting your main point across without alienating the audience.

When to hold your fire. If you sense an impatience among members of the audience, and/or if you are running late, walk off with the arrow in the quiver.

In the next chapter, we'll discuss a vital but frequently ignored aspect of the presentation – the *Post–Presentation Analysis*.

Chapter 22

Post–Presentation Analysis

Almost as counter–intuitive as the *Final Arrow* is conducting a *Post–Presentation Analysis*. One's instinct, after completing what may have been an anxiety–filled, pressure–packed presentation, is to relax and perhaps enjoy a small celebration.

Big mistake. Your senses are alert, your short–term memory in gear. You have just completed an intense, adrenaline–generating experience. If you are never going to make another presentation, then go celebrate, and forget about all the lessons you have just learned, because you'll never need them. But that is the *only* reason you should avoid this after–action report.

Because you are reading this book, I suspect you believe you will be delivering many presentations. One sure way to improve as a presenter is to learn from mistakes, and then use these lessons learned as the springboard to better presentations in the future. The following are the steps to follow to achieve this constant improvement.

22.1 Conduct immediately

Because short term memory is precisely that, you must harvest the lessons of your just–completed presentation within minutes, if at all possible, of completing the presentation. You'll soon forget the specificity of the give–and–take of the presentation, how audience members reacted to you, how you reacted to them, etc.

If you wait even an hour, some particular memory or insight that could prove valuable for future presentations could disappear. Leave the site of the presentation for a relatively quiet place. With a notebook or, better yet, that handy tape recorder you used while practicing, retrace the presentation in your mind.

22.2 Audience questions, objections, and reactions

What were the questions asked, the objections raised to the case you made? Note as well if any hackles were raised by points you made. Who were the audience members most opposed to your position, and why were they opposed? Who were the people in the audience who sided with you?

You can see where this analysis is going – straight to a data base for the next *Murder Board.* Even for a different audience or group of clients, you'll find a similarity of questions raised and provoked by a presentation. You'll be able to share this real–world information with your colleagues participating in a *Murder Board,* making such a practice more focused and realistic.

22.3 Assessment of delivery style and thematic focus

Now you can either pat yourself on the back or kick a little lower. Be frank in your self–assessment, but not overly critical. Look at this post–presentation analysis as an excellent opportunity to hone your skills in this vital area.

Ask colleagues who were present for their frank opinions of what you did well, and where you need to improve. Include this assessment with your written or tape recorded notes.

22.4 A final word on post–presentation analysis

I guarantee that virtually everyone reading this book will not want to conduct such a post–mortem. If, however, you want to maximize the benefits of all the hard work you put into planning, practicing and presenting, you must conduct this analysis immediately after leaving the "stage."

If you do not, you are doomed to reinvent the presentation wheel again and again, and slow your progress toward excelling as a speaker. Isn't excelling as a speaker the reason you bought this book in the first place?

In the final three chapters, we will see how to apply the system taught in this book to special situations.

Part V

Applying the *S3P3 System* to Special Situations

Chapter 23

The Oral Presentation: Key to Winning Government Contracts

The previous pages in this book have outlined a model for organizing the ten gallons of information you have on your specialty into the three–ounce glass of a presentation.

In these final chapters, I want to show how the model can be applied to specific speaking challenges. The next two chapters will show you how to handle yourself in the daunting experience of engaging in a public debate or panel, while this chapter will discuss the procedures to follow when competing for a government contract. This advice can certainly be applied when competing for contracts within the private sector, which is much easier.

Competing for a federal government contract can be bureaucratically frustrating. To paraphrase the late Frank Sinatra in a memorable song, *"if you can make it competing for a government contract, you can make it anywhere."* So we will concentrate on the government process, and

157

you can then extrapolate aspects of the oral presentation process to the private sector.

23.1 The "gag rule" for contractors

Before discussing the process of responding to a government *Request for Proposal (RFP)* let me point out one of the most irritating, and in my judgment, most counter–productive aspects of the government contracting process.

Representatives of companies receiving an RFP are generally prohibited from communicating directly with the very people in the government agency who know what is needed to solve the government's problem. Contractors must instead relay their questions through contracting officers who know little of the substantive needs of the agency. They are of little help in clarifying issues raised in the RFP, and the expression *"the blind leading the blind"* fits well.

23.2 The government contracting process

In recent years, the Federal Government has placed increasing emphasis on the oral presentation in awarding contracts. Additionally, many government agencies are stipulating that only those who will be working on the contract are to be involved with the oral presentation.

This is obviously intended to permit government agency evaluators to have an *eye–to–eye meeting* with those with whom they will be working, thereby resolving issues and questions before the contract is awarded. This new emphasis on the oral presentation has not been greeted with universal acclaim by companies.

Most firms have developed a skilled cadre of proposal writers, and probably feel a bit uneasy about having their economic future riding not on the demonstrated ability of these writers but instead on the speaking skills of engineers and technicians who have not been called on in the past to make marketing presentations. Now, however, the *doers must become sellers.*

23.3   The use of visuals in oral presentations

Some government agencies have also instituted changes in the RFP with respect to how visuals will be employed. These agencies, probably realizing the persuasive capability of *PowerPoint* and other graphics programs, often require that only black–and–white overhead transparencies are to be used.

This may not be good news for Microsoft and other software developers, but it is actually a compliment to the effectiveness of such programs. Evaluators in the agencies imposing this restriction may believe they will be able to concentrate more on the substance and recommendations of the presentation if black–and–white overheads are used, and not be swayed by the remarkable features of computer–generated visuals.

Another restriction dealing with visuals can be counterproductive. The company bidding on the contract, or more likely the group of companies combining their talents into a consortium, are sometimes required to submit the overheads approximately two weeks before the actual presentation.

Evaluators want to have a "heads–up" on the direction the presentation will take, and to see how it tracks with the already–submitted written proposal.

Unfortunately, this early delivery may inhibit the synergistic creativity that can be generated in the run–up to the presentation by people from the diverse backgrounds found within a consortium. Thinking may be "frozen" to the submitted overheads.

Both the government and the consortium lose if this happens, as excellent ideas may not be included in the presentation if they were developed after the visuals were sent to the government. A way to lessen the impact of this problem will be shown later in this chapter.

23.4 Team presentation: Indicator of competence

Delivering an excellent oral presentation does not guarantee a company that it will be awarded the contract, but an indifferent, disorganized and unclear presentation can certainly undermine a company's chances.

Evaluators from the government have a responsibility to get the best buy for the taxpayer's dollar, and may, at least subconsciously, see a correlation between the effectiveness of the team's presentation and how the consortium will accomplish the requirements stipulated in the RFP.

Certain key questions will be in the minds of these evaluators:

1. What is the chemistry between and among team members?

2. Does the team have a clear vision of what the government wants accomplished, or does the presentation suggest the team is still trying to figure out what is required by the RFP?

3. Do the skills of the different companies and individuals complement each other or clash?

4. Is the prime contractor really in charge, or do there appear to be some Prima Donnas among the sub–contractors, suggesting later friction?

5. Does the presentation demonstrate that the consortium has the experience to accomplish the project required by the RFP?

6. Is there a willingness of team members to accept government oversight, or an attitude of "give us the contract, then get out of the way?"

7. Most importantly, does the company/consortium seem genuinely interested in, and demonstrate proven capability to solve, the government's problem?

Technical experts placed in the position of making the oral presentation must strive to demonstrate they are a confident (but not arrogant), competent, and coordinated team.

The model of this book has been the *Three P's System* of *Planning, Practicing,* and *Presenting.* Let's adapt this three–step approach to the task of making a successful, contract–winning oral presentation.

23.5 Planning

As I wrote at the beginning of this book, and reiterated throughout, having a plan on how to achieve your presentation objective is necessary for any presentation. With millions of dollars riding on the strength of an oral presentation, it is imperative. Here are some steps to follow to give you and your company the best chance of winning a lucrative contract.

Read the RFP from the government's perspective. The government has written the RFP to solicit a solution to a problem, and is looking to the private sector for that solution. The government agency also believes it has the ultimate responsibility to the taxpayers, and probably will not look kindly at the consortium that appears resistant to such oversight.

Involve senior management to gain commitment of resources and personnel. Both the prime contractor and the sub–contractors must be willing to expend resources necessary to win the contract. This commitment must be made by senior management of all involved companies, and include making key experts available when required for brain storming and practice sessions, even during the June–August vacation time frame.

Develop an overall theme that is responsive to the RFP. Think of this theme as the lead paragraph in an article in *The Washington Post* or *The New York Times* describing the program to be undertaken. The *3–1–2 System* of *backward planning* described in Chapter 8 will develop focus and thematic unity. When this theme is developed, all presenters must coordinate their presentations so they stay with this theme to achieve clarity and consistency.

23.6 Practicing

Get professional help. The purpose of the government's new emphasis on oral presentations is, of course, to have the people with in–depth knowledge make the presentation, not polished speakers who possess less–detailed knowledge of the RFP requirements.

Still, the team of experts making the clearest and most professional presentation certainly increases its prospects of winning the contract. An outside speaking coach should be brought in to show the technical experts how to make a clear and effective presentation that focuses on the government's needs.

In addition to providing knowledge of the speaking art, this coach will be much more frank in providing constructive criticism to presenters than will coworkers, who, wanting to maintain positive working relationships, may be kinder and gentler in their critiques of presentations in the various *Murder Boards* (see below).

The coach's objective is to blend the techniques of effective presentation skills with the expertise of the presenters. The fusion of these two elements produces contract–winning presentations.

Solve the early visuals problem. If the RFP stipulates that visuals must be delivered early, the potential problem of having the thinking and recommendations/solutions "frozen" to the overheads already sent to the government agency must be taken into account at the outset.

When the visuals are being built, they must (1) have the specificity to permit the evaluators to follow the presentation's general theme, main points, and recommendations, but (2) are sufficiently broad in scope to permit fitting in new ideas generated after the overheads have been submitted. One person should be the coordinator of the visuals to assure consistency.

The *Murder Board.* This simulation, important in virtually all presentations, is invaluable in the run–up to a competitive presentation Such intense practice sessions permit presenters to improve their delivery skills and anticipate questions and objections of the actual evaluators. Some members of the presentation team may resist participating in such intense practice sessions, saying they do not require such play–acting.

These confident (or fearful) people should be reminded of words referred to in Chapter 13 of Albert Einstein: *"What a person does on his own, without being stimulated by the thoughts and experiences of others, is, even in the best cases, rather paltry and monotonous."*

If Einstein believed he needed outside stimulation for his best work, perhaps these reluctant presenters can be convinced they may benefit from this pressure–packed crucible.

The various *Murder Boards*, with fellow members of the presentation team role–playing the government agency evaluators, should be video–taped, and the video–tapes critiqued with little mercy. The following four areas should be the focus of the *Murder Boards*.

Hone the delivery skills of all speakers. The purpose of the oral presentation is to transmit, clearly and persuasively, the vision of the consortium as to how it intends to accomplish the RFP–expressed requirements. The technical experts making the presentation will concentrate on the *What* of the presentation, but they cannot ignore *How* the presenters communicate their ideas to the evaluators.

Improve non–verbals of presenters. Poor eye contact and body language, as well as poor vocal inflection, especially monotone delivery and *"uh's"* and *"y'knows,"* can negatively impact on the way a message is received. We like to think the *Substance* of our presentation is more important than how we look and sound.

Research has shown, however, the overriding importance of non–verbal communication on audiences' perception of both messenger and message. The outside coach earns his or her keep in showing how to blend *Substance* with *Style*.

Don't read from a script. One of the greatest speaking errors of people not accustomed to presenting is to read from a script. Little eye contact is made with the audience, and the thought may occur to the evaluators that this person is reading words written by someone else.

Note cards. 3x5 cards are best because their size precludes writing too much. These "memory joggers" can certainly be used, but speakers should show they own the material.

Don't read the visuals. The evaluators are literate and do not need you to read the words on the screen. Few things alienate audience members more than to have the speaker read verbatim the words on the visuals.

Speakers should reduce to a minimum the text on the visuals during the various *Murder Boards*. To avoid falling into the *reading from the screen trap*, try this drill. Position yourself with your feet pointing at the audience, and at such an angle from the screen that turning to read will cause you discomfort. Don't make the pivot; keep those feet pointing toward the audience.

Use rhetorical devices to reinforce your message. Use of rhetorical devices, or *shortcuts to Eloquence* as I call them in Chapter 16, can add impact to the intellectual content of the message, as well as increase retention by the audience.

Start using them in the practice sessions, and you'll be quite comfortable in the actual presentation. Repetition of key points, done adroitly in cadences of three, has a remarkable ability to cause audience members to remember the speaker's remarks.

The *pause*, especially if it is used as a substitute for *"uh"* and *"y'know,"* likewise tends to reinforce the speaker's words and message. In my workshop, I put special emphasis on learning these and several other techniques. Even inexperienced presenters will appear polished and articulate when they add these weapons to their speaking arsenal.

23.7 Presenting

"Case the joint." If possible, the entire team should visit the room where the presentation will be made before the big day. Observe where the evaluators will sit, where the electrical outlets are located, if there are easels for flip charts (if permitted by the RFP).

If the room lacks curtains or blinds, will sunlight at the time you are scheduled to present wash out the visuals? Because you wish to neither wash out the visuals nor plunge the room into total darkness, can lights immediately in front of a built–in screen be turned off separately?

If driving to the location of the presentation, determine the traffic congestion, time to drive, and parking availability at the time you will be arriving for the presentation. Showing up late could provide the excuse for evaluators to eliminate your team from consideration.

Bring your own projector (and screen if necessary). Overhead projectors vary in how they operate. (Remember that the government may not permit *PowerPoint*.) A team that shows up with its own projector (and a spare bulb) sends a signal that it *has its act together*, Conversely, a team that does not know how to operate the government's projector will appear unprepared (and perhaps not to be trusted to be able to complete the terms of the contract.)

Be ready for the little problems created by visuals, as Murphy's Law has not been repealed. Bringing your own portable screen will permit you to avoid being forced to project your overheads on a built–in screen in front of a bank of lights.

Stand while presenting. Inexperienced presenters will prefer sitting while making the presentation. It may be more comfortable, but the presenter who stands has better presence, better voice control, better eye contact. All *Murder Board* presentations should be made standing to help presenters get used to being on stage.

Stay within time limits stipulated in the RFP. The RFP will normally specify the time allowed for the presentation, and will assess *penalty points* for going beyond these limits. Staying within the specified time limit can be perceived as an indicator of efficiency.

Think of the time limit as a budget. Come in "under budget" and you score points; go "over budget" and you lose points. Literally.

The Question & Answer session. The RFP generally calls for a Q&A session for clarification purposes after the formal presentation. Unless the evaluators say they wish to direct their questions to specific team members, the team leader from the prime contractor should quarterback this session, directing questions to team members according to their respective expertise.

The stress level on presenters will probably be less during the Q & A session because it will take place within the more familiar conversational context. But don't be lulled into a false sense of comfort. Practice the Q & A session.

A Q&A session should be an integral part of the *Murder Board* so as to anticipate the type of questions likely to be asked. The actual Q&A session is where the evaluator's doubts and questions can be resolved, key points driven home by the presenters in their answers. It can certainly increase the comfort level of the evaluators that the team presenting will be able to do the job called for by the RFP.

23.8 Some final advice

If your competitors are improving the presentation skills of their technical experts because of the importance they attach to oral presentations, while you rely on your superior ideas, programs, and experience, you may find your firm losing millions of dollars.

A small investment in presentations training, therefore, can pay large dividends when lucrative contracts are awarded.

The next two chapters provide the strategy and tactics to deal with "difficult audiences," and can be read in the context of debates, panel appearances and certainly sales presentations.

Chapter 24

Dealing with Difficult Audiences: *The Strategy*

Unless you are a motivational speaker or teller of humorous stories, you will, alas, sometimes have the experience of speaking to audience members who would rather jeer than cheer.

The experience is definitely not fun, I can tell you from the personal experience of speaking to scores of such audiences when defending and debating controversial policies for the government. You'll find, however, that confronting such audiences will make you a better speaker. The old adage *"What does not kill you makes you stronger"* is particularly apt.

There is a certain nostalgia connected with writing this chapter. The first article I ever wrote for publication after retiring from the Army was titled *Taming the Hostile Audience*, published in the *Training & Development Journal*, the magazine of the American Society for Training and Development.

It was in that article that I outlined for the first time the principles that have been the mainstay of my executive training program, and which are embedded throughout this book.

A speaker using his/her credibility and knowledge when addressing a supportive audience is merely reinforcing the audience's existing views. It is a far greater challenge to sell a point of view to people predisposed to disagree, or at least containing a significant and perhaps vociferous element which is opposed to the issue being advocated by the speaker.

Many of you will be tempted to stop reading at this point, thinking *"I'll not be participating in any debates or confrontational panels in front of difficult audiences."* Not so fast.

Every presentation you make to prospective clients, or to a Board of Directors, or even at a PTA, can soon evolve into a debate when demanding, critical and questioning people in the audience challenge your facts.

24.1 Why some audiences can be difficult

We live in an increasingly high–tempo, fast–moving, information–laden, real–time age, and the pace is picking up. Audiences are knowledgeable, critical, impatient, and demanding.

No longer are "touchy–feely" speaking skills sufficient – more than a friendly demeanor, positive attitude, and lots of eye contact are required.

Presenters in the 21st Century must blend substantive mastery, focused structure, and stylistic elegance to a degree not required previously. In today's contentious business and government climate, adversarial panels, debates, and presentations on controversial issues are more the rule than the exception.

Speakers representing corporations and government agencies are likely to find themselves not just speaking to hostile audiences, but in rhetorical combat in panels or debates with adversaries who have the support of an audience strongly opposed to the position of the government or corporate representative.

Public debates and panels on controversial issues are becoming common. Perhaps it has been the institutionalization of Presidential and other political debates over the last several years that has led to this state of affairs. Perhaps there is a "Roman Coliseum" desire that craves the clash of ideas, issues and rivals.

A debate or confrontational panel means sharing the platform with a person or persons opposed to you, perhaps with an audience acting as cheerleader for these opponent(s). You will then know how the Christians felt as they looked at the hungry lions.

24.2 Dealing with demanding, skeptical audiences

To be an effective presenter under such circumstances, whether in high–stakes sales or contract presentations, or in a debate or panel, a flexible *blue print* must be developed for transferring information and perceptions from the speaker's mind to the minds of audience members.

When facing a skeptical audience, speakers must keep in mind that the information they are presenting is not going into empty vessels, but is mixing with the preconceived opinions and biases of audience members.

Consequently, anticipating how audience members will react, and what lines of attack any opponent(s) will follow, is an absolute necessity. It is, in fact, foolish to ignore this advice. Yet many people take the fatalistic view that there is no way people with their minds made up can be turned around.

There are two fundamental requirements for success in presenting to tough, skeptical or even hostile audiences. These requirements are (1) the need for rapport and (2) common ground with the audience.

A presenter can connect with even a skeptical audience by showing that he or she shares certain views with members of the audience. Without rapport and common ground, there is no chance of success.

24.3 Fundamental one: Develop rapport

To have any chance of converting audience members to your point of view, you must get them to like or respect you. One way is to establish personal contact, perhaps by phone, with key members of the audience well before the presentation. By doing so, you'll be able to gain additional intelligence on why these people are opposed to you.

Arrive early at the location of the debate/panel/presentation so you can have conversations with people who are probably opposed to you. Learn more about their concerns, just why they are opposed to the position you are advocating.

They in turn will see you as a human being, not a remote corporate figure. During the actual presentation, mention the names of the people with whom you have conferred. Nothing is so sweet to the human ear as the sound of his or her name, especially if it is mentioned positively before others.

After the presentation, don't rush off. Stay around for *post–speech mingling*. You may be able to influence a few more people by staying and answering their questions.

Audience members will have a more favorable perception of a speaker who stays to chat, even after being pelted with tough questions. If you have done a good job during the presentation, only to rush off, you squander an excellent opportunity to reinforce your message.

24.4   Fundamental two: Establish common ground

Rarely are issues so black–and–white that no area of agreement can be found. In fact, even in the most heated political debates, there is normally consensus on the end to be achieved, only disagreement on the means to reach that end.

To reach some common ground with a difficult audience, build on the rapport you have gained by emphasizing the positive aspects of the position of the audience, and where you agree. Even at a high level of abstraction, such as a belief in democracy or the free market system, it at least puts you and the audience on the same page, even if it is a small page.

After establishing that there are points of agreement, you can then move to the arguments supporting your position. Present these arguments, if at all possible, within the context of where you and the audience agree.

A technique I used in facing audiences initially opposed to the position I was advocating was to acknowledge that we in Washington had done a poor job of articulating the fundamentals of our policy, and I could understand why so many people in the audience were opposed to this policy. I would then say I hoped to fill in some of those gaps with my presentation.

In this way, I was providing audience members with the opportunity to "save face," changing their mind as a result of the new information I had presented. Remember that no one wants to admit they were wrong, and you cannot persuade people to change their mind; they must persuade themselves.

24.5 Six strategic *Knows*

The six strategic *Knows* outlined in the following pages provide a strategic framework for challenging speaking situations. Those preparing for a presentation or debate on a controversial subject will have all the normal anxieties of speaking in front of any group, plus the real possibility of public humiliation.

These speakers have two options: (1) Take the fatalistic view to just show the corporate or government flag and try to lessen the damage, believing there is no possibility of changing the individual or collective minds of the audience, or (2) Be so well–prepared, through use of the strategic guidelines in the following pages, that the tables can be turned on both biased audience members and opponents so as to actually *win*, or at least appear to not have lost.

Practicing is important for any presentation, but absolutely vital for those occasions when matching wits with others in the debate or panel format. You may feel confident in your ability to think fast, but it is invariably better to follow a systematic methodology that hones the ability to anticipate audience reactions and develop responses based on this intelligence.

This strategy of the six *Knows* is not classroom theory. It is the product of my actual experience in scores of such encounters in the *real world*. It has been tested, has worked for me, and will work for you.

24.6 *Know* your material from both sides

This is the *First Principle of speaking*. The truly outstanding speaker follows the observation of the great British statesman Benjamin Disraeli, who said, *"Eloquence is the child of knowledge."*

A speaker or debater must have mastery of the material being discussed. But it is not enough merely to have in–depth knowledge of the issue from your point of view; you must know the subject as well *from the other side* so you can anticipate and counter objections.

To provide focus to your research and practice, question every fact and assertion in your argument. Examine the basic assertions from the standpoint of an *opposing* audience.

Substantive, verifiable data is the *Logos* – arguments that appeal to the mind – of Aristotle's *On Rhetoric*. To go before a skeptical audience, especially if you are facing opponents in a debate or panel, with only superficial knowledge, is both reckless and foolish.

You will see below how the remaining strategic *Knows* and the implementing tactics in the next chapter will save you a lot of grief and potential embarrassment.

24.7. *Know* your objective – stay on message

The speaker or debater must have a clearly defined objective in mind – what he or she wishes the audience to do. For a debate or panel, it is even more important to keep an eye on the endgame – providing the audience members with a rationale to modify their view, despite the arguments to the contrary made by opponent(s).

Keeping your objective in mind is just as necessary in a sales presentation as it is in an internal business presentation, such as a meeting of the Board of Directors. The *opponent(s)* could be hard–to–sell prospective clients, or members of the Board whose ox you may be goring. Know what their counter–arguments and objections will be, and prepare to trump them.

In an emotionally charged meeting, with senior executives being critical of your position, or in a debate with opponent(s) playing to the biases of the audience, even the strongest–willed speaker may come to doubt the validity of his or her position in the face of unrelenting attack.

Having a well–defined objective is the necessary first step. How does one do this? By internalizing the *3–1–2 System* of structuring the presentation, covered earlier in Chapter 8.

24.8 *Know* the format in a debate

Most public, non–academic debates last two hours. Each speaker is given twenty minutes to state his/her case, and ten minutes for rebuttal. That leaves approximately one hour for questions and answers from the audience.

Always coordinate in advance with the program organizer to determine the time and format. Most importantly, determine how questions are to be asked by the audience, and whether debaters and panelists can question or challenge each other.

If microphones are to be placed in the aisles, allowing people with questions to line up, it generally works to the disadvantage of the *establishment speaker.* Ask (or demand) the moderator/program organizer to change the procedure so that questioners are recognized at random by the moderator and then invited to walk to the microphones.

This lessens the likelihood that a vociferous group opposing your position will be able to capture the microphones. This request should be made at the time the debate/panel is scheduled. Waiting until the event may be too late.

The *Crossfire* and *Lehrer Newshour* television news programs have been very influential in establishing a norm by which audiences judge debates and panels. Having appeared on both programs, I can say with some confidence that the former is intellectual mud–wrestling, while the latter is thoughtful discourse. Both can be informative and useful. The former is more entertaining, the latter perhaps more fruitful.

It is better to seek the *Newshour* format in front of an audience opposed to you, because the *Crossfire* format could cause the audience to get out of hand, inflamed by the remarks of your opponent.

24.9 *Know* the audience's cognitive dissonance

You must never forget in the heat of battle that it is the people *in the audience* that you are attempting to convert, *not your opponent(s).* Most importantly, be aware of the role that *Cognitive Dissonance*, covered in Chapter 5, plays in an audience's perceptions.

Speakers confronted with an audience composed of people who apparently *have their minds made up* must always remember that facts alone will not persuade, and they must be able to furnish an answer to the question *"Why should I alter my position?"*

177

Most importantly, let me reiterate the importance of allowing these people to *save face* and not have to admit to themselves that they were *wrong*. Don't tell them your purpose is to *persuade* or *convince* them. Share new information in such a manner that they can come to the support of your position *on their own.*

24.10 *Know* your opponents

If you are involved in a debate or panel, what are the qualifications and biases of your opponent(s) on the dais with you, or in the audience? If they have published or spoken on the issue being discussed, analyze the presentation, article or book carefully.

This will provide you with your opponent's *game plan*, and enable you to develop counter–arguments. Consult with anyone who has debated these people, or presented to this group, in order to determine idiosyncrasies such as low boiling point, tendency to make sweeping generalizations, etc.

Knowing this in advance will not only be tactically advantageous, it will also reduce the *fear of the unknown*, making your opponent, or potential adversaries in the audience, seem more human, less omniscient, and eminently *defeatable.*

Even experienced speakers can be intimidated in advance by an opponent's reputation. The more you know about an adversary's background, biases and speaking style, the better able you will be to exploit weak points. *And everyone has weak points, including you!*

24.11 *Know* your vulnerabilities

The worst situation you can encounter in a debate, panel or presentation is to have an opponent or audience member make a devastating comment reflecting on your credibility or the validity of the position you are advocating, and you find yourself speechless because you have not anticipated this charge and developed a response.

When you know you have a significant vulnerability, acknowledge this Achilles' heel *before* your opponent has the chance to do so. He or she will be surprised if you bring the issue up first, as much of his or her strategy may have been based on a devastating revelation.

The importance of candor, even if it means taking a short–term hit, has been articulated by famed defense attorney Gerry Spence. He has never lost a jury trial, perhaps in large measure because of what he wrote in his best selling 1995 book *How to Argue and Win Every Time:*

> *"Concession is a proper method both to establish credibility and to structure a successful argument successfully. I always concede at the outset what is true even if it is detrimental to my argument. Concession coming from your mouth is not nearly as hurtful as an exposure coming from your opponent's."*

If you have the opportunity to speak first, follow Spence's advice, putting your vulnerability in perspective. The audience will consider this a sign of your honesty. You will be seen as not being evasive, your credibility will be enhanced, and your opponent will have been out–maneuvered, for his or her broadside will have been preempted.

179

In preparing for your debate or presentation, list three vulnerabilities of your position that you would *not like* to be brought up, and develop succinct counter–arguments. With thought, and an intensive *Murder Board–Mock Debate* (see the following chapter) with knowledgeable colleagues, you can probably frame a credible response, appear not surprised, lessen the impact of your opponent's *hit*, and display coolness under fire.

Keeping your response short, focused and "punchy" will add to your credibility, as long as it is factual. Long, complex explanations may not be understood, and you may be perceived as being both defensive and evasive. Make sure, of course, that you have thought out the line of reasoning you will use to reframe and defuse the vulnerability so you do not make it worse. Remember to not appear to be discounting or downplaying the serious nature of the issue. If the audience believes it to be serious, so should you.

In the next chapter, we'll look at specific tactics to help you either *win* these intellectual fire–fights, or at least appear to not have lost.

Chapter 25

Dealing with Difficult Audiences: *The Tactics*

The strategic advice in the preceding chapter provides the framework for your potentially confrontational presentation or debate. Below are ten tactical implementers which, if followed, should enable you to come out on top in this most daunting speaking challenge.

25.1 Tactic one: Be prudently aggressive

A debate, panel or presentation must be approached with the positive attitude *"I am going to succeed."* To enter this form of intellectual combat with a fatalistic, overly cautious, limit–the–damage strategy such as then–Senator Quayle's coaches adopted is to almost guarantee failure (see Chapter 11).

Playing for the win as opposed to *playing not to lose* is a hallmark of successful sports teams and speakers alike. This is not to say that one should be foolhardy. The key is to be fully aware of your own vulnerabilities and those of your opponent(s) so you can minimize damage to your position while inflicting maximum damage to the position being advocated by your opponent(s).

Look for errors of logic in the argument of your opponent(s) that you can exploit, but also be prudent to see if you are being set up, just as you would want to lay an ambush (see 25.6 below) for your opponent.

25.2 Tactic two: The *Mock Debate–Murder Board*

The key to effective preparation for a debate or demanding presentation is the ability to anticipate opposing arguments to your position. Nothing will aid you more than a no–holds–barred *Murder Board–Mock Debate*. Review the advice provided in Chapters 13 and 14.

I strongly recommend a tough practice session before *any* difficult, chips–on–the–line presentation, but it is virtually mandatory to have one before a debate or presentation in which you know you will encounter strong opposition to your view, unless you take some perverse joy in being humiliated in public.

Charges, accusations and misrepresentations may be flying fast and furious, and no debater or speaker should count solely on his or her ability to think fast.

It is far better to have anticipated charges by your opponents(s) and developed answers in advance as a result of an intense practice session. Make your mistakes in front of allies who can help you correct these errors of style and substance so you can both score points against your adversary's vulnerabilities and rebut effectively those assaults against your own.

If you have the time, consider playing the role of your debate opponent. Alternatively, have a colleague assume your role as you sit in the audience observing. If your were your opponent, how you would attack? This will allow you to develop better counter–arguments. *Standing in the adversary's shoes* can pay immense dividends by allowing you to gain a better grasp of your own vulnerabilities and those of your opponent(s).

25.3 Tactic three: Stay cool and composed

In debates and high stakes presentations, it is very understandable for the speaker defending a position at variance with the collective view of an aggressive and vociferous audience – and opponent(s) – to lose his or her temper. Don't let yourself be goaded into a shouting match with either audience members or opponents.

When someone shouts, lower your voice, and speak in a strong, slow, deliberate tone, maintaining eye contact with the shouter. Don't allow yourself to appear to be either intimidated or angered, although a touch of righteous indignation can demonstrate to the audience that you are human.

Think of yourself as the thermostat of an air conditioning unit. When the "heat" of debate and disagreement increases, kick in the cooling mechanism rather than respond in kind to an accusation, which is analogous to turning up the heat in an already over–heated room.

Keep in mind that an audience attending such a public *clash of ideas* is looking for validation of their opinions, and your opponent(s) are reinforcing these opinions. If you can remain composed and unruffled, maintain focus, and not allow yourself to be provoked, you maintain control. You cannot control either your opponent(s) or your audience. You can only control yourself, *and you must.*

25.4 Tactic four: Disguised rebuttal

Unless the pre–debate analysis of your vulnerabilities and/or the *Murder Board–Mock Debate* dictate that you must preempt a charge by going first, it is tactically better to speak second. Policy issues often turn on a debater's ability to *counter–punch* or respond to charges/accusations made by the opponent's *opening statement*. An effective simulation practice will enhance your ability to do so.

The debater going second has the opportunity to use his/her opening statement as a *disguised rebuttal*, perhaps being able to undermine the main points made by the opponent who has spoken first. Moreover, by going second, you have the opportunity to make the final rebuttal, implanting your key arguments at the end and forcing your opponent to try recouping in the Q & A session.

25.5 Tactic five: Stay within your evidence

During the give–and–take of a debate or a boardroom presentation, participants may be tempted to go beyond the hard, factual evidence that is the underpinning of their argument. This tendency to exaggerate can occur as easily to a person who is *winning* as one who is being pummeled by an opponent or the audience.

The former can stem from overconfidence, the latter from frustration. An analogy or metaphor may be stretched beyond its limits, or a conclusion stated that is simply not supported by the facts. This can destroy the credibility established up to that point, and provide a lucrative target for your opponent(s). Conversely, if your opponent goes beyond the evidence, you can damage his credibility with a well–placed rebuttal.

In baseball, a batter who goes for the home run is just as likely to strike out, while the hitter who goes for the single is less likely to miss the ball. Babe Ruth, although hitting 714 home runs, also struck out 1,330 times. Don't swing for the fence, or you may snatch defeat from the jaws of victory.

25.6   Tactic six: Seek "ambush" opportunities

When faced with a hostile audience supporting a knowledgeable foe, a bit of *gamesmanship* may be necessary. You can undermine the confidence audience members have in the expertise of your opponent – their champion – if you demonstrate that he or she has made a false statement or perhaps used dated or unreliable sources.

How do you induce your opponent to make this mistake? By counting on his or her overconfidence, and your knowledge of the line of argument he or she has made in the past, perhaps in a previous speech or article. If your research has shown the point made in the past by your adversary will not bear up under scrutiny, make a statement that lures the opponent into resurrecting that previous assertion. Then you, citing specific sources, prove how erroneous is his or her position.

If possible, work out this "ambush scenario" in your *Murder Board–Mock Debate*. A skillful and apparently spontaneous revelation of your opponent's blunder can demonstrate to members of the audience that their advocate is either speaking with forked tongue or is not the expert they had believed him or her to be.

With such a victory, you may start to win converts to your side by creating cognitive dissonance (Chapter 5) within the audience.

25.7   Tactic seven:
Selective rebuttal and the "T" form

Given the amount of material to be covered in a contentious debate, panel, or conflictive presentation, and the limited time available, you will never be able to rebut all of the charges and misrepresentations made against your position.

An intensive *Murder Board–Mock Debate* will help you anticipate many of your opponent's main lines of argument and thereby develop counter–arguments. But there will undoubtedly be unanticipated points raised to which you will have to respond in the heat of battle. So another bit of *gamesmanship* will prove helpful – the "T" form.

Before the debate/panel, draw a large "T" on a piece of note paper. During the debate/panel, write as many of the charges/accusations made by your opponent(s) in the left column. Write rebuttals that you *can* make in the right column, with as much credible source data as you can muster.

When your turn comes for rebuttal, you can state in a confident voice, *"My opponent has made a number of errors, but time permits me to address only the most egregious of them."*

You appear to have answers for all the accusations, and, had you only the time, the information to expose in its entirety the flawed logic of your opponent. The risk, of course, is that you may be given the extra time you lamented not having, and you cannot deliver. But time is scarce, and the ploy will probably work. Alternatively, you can just ignore the charges you cannot respond to adequately, and rebut only those that you can.

25.8   Tactic eight: Non–verbals unique to debate

During a debate or a public meeting, participants are always *on stage*. When your opponent is speaking, audience members will be watching to see how you react. Any defensive body language, such as a grimace reacting to a charge made by your opponent, will all be noted and some detrimental meaning attached.

Positive non–verbals can help you plant doubt about the veracity of the opponent's charge, such as a subtle lifting of an eyebrow to register incredulity. On the other hand, negative, defensive non–verbals send the signal to the audience that your opponent has hit a nerve.

If you appear bored or indifferent, you may be considered impolite or arrogant by the audience. The best facial expression is one of interest in your opponent's remarks. A *slight* shaking of the head in apparent disbelief can be effective in sending the signal that what the opponent has said is not true. Again, don't overdo it, or audience members may consider you rude.

Always maintain erect posture. Don't slouch, and listen attentively to your opponent(s). When making your presentation, concentrate on eye contact with the audience (which means less reliance on notes) to show that you are a master of the subject, not a "talking dog" sent out to bark a party line.

Using the lectern is completely acceptable, but moving away from it, especially if your opponent stays behind it, shows that you are the one who has command of the material.

Never, ever look at your watch the way President George Bush did in the second presidential debate in 1992. He may have wanted to know how much time was left to get in key points. Unfortunately for him, the

187

perception of millions of would–be voters watching on television was that he was on the defensive, very uncomfortable, and was checking to see how much more abuse he had to endure, much as a fighter against the ropes would want to know how much time was left in the round.

In a debate/panel in front of a skeptical or hostile audience, looking openly at your watch may be perceived as a sign of weakness. It is far better to "sneak a peek" while appearing to be taking notes. You certainly want to know how much time is left to make your last point. Just be discreet.

25.9 Tactic nine: Reverse quoting

Buttressing your argument by quoting an authority identified with *your* position will do little to sway an audience opposed to you. Providing a quotation supporting your view, or at least undercutting the position of your opponent(s), from an authoritative source *normally identified with opposition to your position,* can shake the resolve of the audience, sowing doubt with respect to the position being pressed by your opponent(s).

The key is finding credible sources which provide this information. For a debate, panel or presentation dealing with a political issue, a valuable source would be *The Congressional Record.* Because members of Congress are typically cautious in adopting controversial positions, they will frequently give speeches that reflect ambiguous, sometimes even contradictory, positions. Journals such as *Foreign Affairs* and *Foreign Policy* likewise are an excellent source of information from recognized authorities, as are the op–ed pages of major newspapers.

For business issues, publications such as *The Wall Street Journal, Fortune, Forbes, Business Week, Vital Speeches* etc., provide a rich source of quotations and information. All of the above sources have web sites, many with archives to help you search for the precise information needed.

A word of caution: In quoting, read the entire speech/interview so as not to be vulnerable to the charge of taking information out of context.

25.10 Tactic ten: Using "footnotes"

Your credibility is enhanced when you can provide precise, factual data supported by known and objective sources, as opposed to stating a mere assertion.

Whenever possible, use primary sources. If you use a secondary source, and your opponent uses the primary source for the data, he or she may be able to imply you drew an invalid conclusion or took information out of context.

You, of course, can employ the same technique against your opponent. Use numbers and survey data when possible, and make sure your information is the latest available.

It would be embarrassing to quote one set of figures and have your opponent(s) provide more current information that contradicts you. Do not become the victim of an ambush: *Be the "ambusher."*

Have these oral footnotes placed on cards, perhaps color coded, when you prepare for a debate or panel. The knowledge you possess on an important issue may go for naught if you cannot, in the heat of a debate or a pressure–packed presentation, retrieve the devastating rebuttal from a credible source.

189

25.11 Final words on dealing with *difficult* audiences

The advice in this and the previous chapter should serve you well in any speaking challenge, but especially when facing an audience more inclined to jeer than cheer.

There is no greater challenge in the field of speaking than the debate or panel with informed, passionate adversaries in front of an audience that at least initially shares the views of these opponent(s). Close behind in difficulty is the presentation to clients, or a boardroom presentation in which the speaker is "selling" a controversial project, defending an unpopular issue, or delivering "bad news."

Many people are inclined to take a fatalistic position at the prospect of dealing with such a challenge. *But that attitude is self−defeating.* If you have a strong belief in the position you are advocating, devote the time to plan and practice, using the tested advice contained in these pages.

Emotions play an important role with any audience, but it is still verifiable, factual data that persuades reasonable people to come to your side. Keep in mind that *you* will not persuade an audience; *the audience must persuade itself.* Allow audience members to "save face" by providing backing for your position with oral footnotes, and with information they did not have prior to listening to you.

A debate or presentation before audience members who disagree with you is a wonderful opportunity to "write on their brains" with the thoughts you wish them to accept, retain and act upon. Calmly match your arguments to those of your opponent(s) and you may be able to expose the falsity of their position. Just remember to maintain your composure, avoid personal attacks, and remember your objective for the debate or presentation—*what you want your audience to do as a result of listening to your argument.*

Finally, always keep in mind that "winning" does not mean scoring debating points, humiliating your opponent, or alienating a questioner with a patronizing answer. Do this and you will leave the debate/panel/presentation *without* having opened any minds, perhaps in the process losing support for your position. You do not want to win a battle and lose a war.

Chapter 26

My *Final Arrow*

> *"If, through some inscrutable act of providence I were to lose all my faculties save one, I would wish to retain the gift of speech, for with it I would soon regain all the others."*
>
> **Senator Daniel Webster**

Those words of Daniel Webster may appear familiar. They should. It's the same memorable and accurate phrase with which I started the Preface to this book. They bear repeating, and my *Final Arrow* is the appropriate place to deliver them to you once more.

Webster, one of the greatest statesmen and orators of the 19th Century, recognized the importance of speaking ability as a "multiplier" of our other talents. My goal in this book has not only been to drive home that point, but to show you a *shortcut* to maximize your ability to use the spoken word.

This book has provided you a systematic, proven method to (1) *plan, practice,* and *present* with a persuasive focus and thematic unity, (2) mesh your objective as a speaker with your audience's concerns and needs, and (3) anticipate objections and questions from audience members so you can develop effective counter–arguments and answers before the presentation. The *shortcut* approach developed in this book has worked for me. It has worked for participants in my workshops. It will work for you.

Two sayings relevant to the understanding of the speaking art worth remembering are: *"The second business of any business is the making of presentations,"* and *"People may not remember a good presentation, but they rarely forget a bad one."* The system you have learned in this book will help you avoid "making a bad one."

Remember that clarity and brevity are fundamental responsibilities of the presenter, who must both *get to the point* and frame his or her argument in terms that are understandable to the audience.

If your audience does not grasp your message, it is your fault. No one can say, *"I was very clear, but they just didn't get it."* Audiences must persuade themselves, and it is up to the presenter to frame the presentation so audience members see their interests being served by the argument presented by the speaker.

Let me close this book with an observation from the birthplace of speech training–ancient Greece. The Greeks of that day, even while admiring the speaker with the stentorian voice, dramatic gesture and clever turn of phrase, nevertheless realized the purpose of any presentation was to cause audience members to take the action the speaker wished them to take. So it was said, in comparing the greatest speaker of the day with one who had lived many years before:

> *"When Demosthenes speaks, people say 'how well he speaks'. But when Pericles spoke, people said, 'Let us march.'"*

Index

197

Made in the USA
Charleston, SC
27 April 2013

THE SHORTCUT
TO
PERSUASIVE PRESENTATIONS

by Larry Tracy

THE SHORTCUT TO PERSUASIVE PRESENTATIONS

by Larry Tracy

Published in the United States of America by
Imprint Books
An affiliate of BookSurge LLC
5341 Dorchester Road, Suite 16
North Charleston, SC 29418
www.booksurge.com

Cover design: Cathi Stevenson
(cstevenson@accessible.net)

ISBN 1–59109–702–9

Printed in the United States of America